Acclaim for
"Kids Pick Up on Everything"

"David Code's book does a great service for families, providing insights that promise better health for our kids. He sets out to teach parents, in a compassionate and accessible way, how their stress may affect their children's health, without laying on blame or guilt. David's book is a great way to get the message to parents, starting a dialogue that absolutely needs to begin now."
-Rosalind J. Wright, MD, Professor of Medicine, Harvard Medical School, and Principal Investigator, Asthma Coalition (ACCESS) Project

"The stress levels in our society are having a profound effect on our children's health. Parents urgently need to know how they can reduce toxic stress in their families, and David Code is the first to translate this medical research into an easy, readable book that can help parents reduce their stress and raise healthier kids. I recommend this book highly."
-Moshe Szyf, Professor, McGill Medical School, and Co-founder, The Sackler Institute for Epigenetics and Psychobiology

"The effect of stress on a child's development is a rapidly emerging topic in medicine, and David explains the latest research in a very entertaining and compelling way. His message is essential to all parents."
-David Beversdorf, MD, Chair of the Interdisciplinary Neuroscience Program, University of Missouri Medical School

"David Code elegantly and accessibly describes the toll parents' stressful lifestyles take on children's health. In doing so, he gives parents permission to simplify their stressful lives—and promote their children's health in the process. I recommend this book to parents in any stage of their parenting journey."
-Nicole Talge, Research Associate, Dept. of Epidemiology, Michigan State University

"David Code's book is right on the money with his analysis and conclusions. David's work may conflict with mainstream psychology or the drug company establishment, but he has been careful to back up his hypothesis with expert opinions from researchers. What makes his book a gift to parents are his examples of how couples can keep the enjoyment in their lives and decrease the stress. Parents need to know how we can fight today's epidemic in child disorders, and David Code has given us a simple, clear strategy."
-James Serene, MD, Professor, Penn State Hershey Medical School

Note to Readers

This publication contains the opinions and ideas of its author. It is intended to provide helpful and informative material on the subjects addressed in the publication. It is sold with the understanding that the author and publisher are not engaged in rendering medical, health, or any other kind of personal professional services in the book. The reader should consult his or her medical, health, or other competent professional before adopting any of the suggestions in this book or drawing inferences from it.

The author and publisher specifically disclaim all responsibility for any liability, loss, or risk, personal or otherwise, which is incurred as a consequence, directly or indirectly, of the use and application of any of the contents of this book.

Kids Pick Up on
EVERYTHING

How Parental Stress Is Toxic to Kids

DAVID CODE

ISBN 978-1-4663-0003-3

Table of Contents

PART ONE
HOW A PARENT'S STRESS GETS UNDER A CHILD'S SKIN

CHAPTER 1

CHAPTER 2

How Kids Pick Up On Everything, Part 1—In the Womb

CHAPTER 3

How Kids Pick Up On Everything, Part 2—After a Child is Born

CHAPTER 4

How Parental Stress Affects a Child's Body—Epigenetics

CHAPTER 5

Parental Stress Affects Almost Every Child—It's Just a Matter of Degree

CHAPTER 6

Stress Outside the Womb: Vulnerable Child Syndrome

PART TWO
THE MOTHER IS NOT TO BLAME: WHY DID STRESS BECOME A RISK FACTOR NOW?

CHAPTER 7

Our Dwindling Social Networks Leave Parents More Stressed Than Ever

PART THREE

PRACTICAL STRATEGIES TO HELP YOU RAISE HEALTHY KIDS BY RELAXING AND SOCIALIZING MORE

CHAPTER 12

Introduction

My father was a farmer, and so was his father. I was born on a dusty farm under the big sky of the Canadian prairie, and as the youngest of seven children, I've always been a student of family dynamics. It didn't take a village to raise us—we were a village. Our nearest neighbor lived more than a mile away, the nearest school was thirteen miles away, and winter temperatures could plunge to 50 degrees below zero. So, in that big farmhouse on the barren plains of Saskatchewan, we made our own community. I remember one Christmas vacation when my older brothers and sisters returned home with their partners and children, and we had nineteen people staying in our house—with only one bathroom.

When I was eighteen, my study of family dynamics took quite a leap, from the waving wheat fields of Saskatchewan to the ivy halls of Yale University, Princeton Seminary, and abroad. My fascination with families has now taken me to over fifty different cultures around the globe, where I've stayed with families in twenty countries on five continents. I learned Japanese, Russian, and French so I could explore these exotic cultures, watch the people living their lives, and understand their stories in their own language.

People open up to me because I'm fascinated by their stories, and during my travels, folks from all over the world have invited me into the inner sanctum of their families, as a friend and confidant. I've joined a family eating spicy morsels of snake in a tiny apartment in Shanghai, and attended a Russian-Jewish funeral in Moscow. I've worried with an Indian couple over their daughter's marriage, and picked dates with families on a windy desert farm in Israel. Everywhere I went, couples still loved, parents still worried, and children still wanted to make their parents proud.

Observing families abroad has been a valuable experience, yet equally important has been the chance to temporarily step outside my own culture. A fish does not notice the water in which it swims, but my years as a fish out of water in other countries gave me an outsider's perspective on the turbulent emotional waters in which American families swim every day.

For all the similarities among families around the globe, I discovered something about American families that was unique—and not pretty.

Since I grew up with few resources, I always assumed what many others assume: Families with more money and education must be more secure, more relaxed and just plain happier. But when I was ordained as an Episcopal minister in 2003 and served two wealthy parishes near New York City, I was surprised at what I found.

The wealthy families I counseled almost seemed to suffer more. For example, a successful graphic designer had a daughter with ADHD who had been rejected by several private schools she had applied to. An entrepreneur practiced attachment-parenting with her son for years, including "babywearing" the child on her shoulder or back, and sleeping with him. But her son constantly threw tantrums, and his parents later divorced. Several successful company presidents had children who barely finished high school. Even the relatively normal families I visited often had children with allergies, asthma, learning disabilities, ADHD, or mood disorders, and many were on medication.

This made no sense to me. These kids had well-educated, well-intentioned, self-sacrificing parents who were doing what the experts told them to do: shower your kids with love and attention, help them find and pursue their inner passions, never raise your voice, protect your child at school and defend them on the playground, etc. Yet, their children weren't turning out as expected. Why would kids with loving, dedicated, successful parents and all their advantages end up just as troubled as children with much fewer resources?

One clue was that in many of the homes I visited, the stress was palpable and many couples had drifted apart emotionally. As I listened to parents' kitchen-table confessions, I felt a kind of frenetic, jangly tension that was so thick in the room that one could almost see it. I assumed, like most people would, that these households were tense because their child's problem had left everyone on edge.

Then, I read something that made me look at these families differently.

A psychiatrist named Murray Bowen had conducted an experiment in the 1950's at the National Institute of Mental Health, observing how schizophrenic youth interacted with their families. For 18 months or more, several patients lived with their entire families in a ward where Bowen and his staff could observe and record their behaviors 24/7.

How brilliant, I thought: he observed our species the way Jane Goodall observed our chimp cousins in Tanzania!

As Bowen observed and compared the behavior of these families, a certain pattern emerged. He described *"a striking emotional distance between the parents in all the families. We have called this the 'emotional divorce'…. When either parent becomes more invested in the patient than in the other parent, the psychotic process [in their child] becomes intensified."* In other words, the parents didn't drift apart because they were too busy caring for a schizophrenic child. Rather, the drifting apart of their marriage came first, and it had somehow affected their child's mental health.

I wasn't sure what to make of Dr. Bowen's quirky little experiment, but his concept of the "emotional divorce" forever changed my pastoral counseling to families. For the first time, I noticed my own assumptions and began to question them.

Like most people, I had assumed that a child's health or behavioral problem makes a family tense, which of course it does. But now I asked myself, "What if that couple was tense even before the problem, and their tension somehow contributed to the child's symptoms? If the old saying is true that kids pick up on everything, what if there's some kind of mind-body connection between a parent's anxious mind and a child's sensitive body?"

I began to ask doctors, nurses, teachers and therapists about this mind-body connection between parent and child, and they poured out stories of how overwhelmed they feel by today's seeming epidemic of stressed-out parents and troubled children. As I continued to read more medical studies and interview more experts, my conviction that there is a mind-body connection between a parent's mind and a child's body became stronger. It almost seemed as though children become barometers for their parents' state of mind. Could it be that children are "canaries in the coal mine," indicating when a family's levels of stress have become toxic?

The answer is yes. Here is what every parent needs to know:

1) Kids pick up on everything, especially our stress and anxiety;

2) This happens both in the womb and throughout childhood;

3) The mind-body connection is a primal, instinctive link between every parent and child;

4) This mind-body connection contributes to problems in every family—it's just a question of degree: from colic and food allergies to asthma and autism;

5) This pattern is already epidemic in America, and it's getting worse;

6) This is not the mother's or father's fault. Today's parents are more stressed-out because our social support networks are dwindling, and we don't realize that, as our isolation increases, it drives up our stress levels.

I feel a tremendous sense of urgency in getting my message out to parents, because every day lost is another child growing up with disorders that could have been reduced or even prevented. Asthma now affects 1 child in 10, as does ADHD. The national prevalence of autism almost doubled from 2002 to 2006, and now it is 1 out of 110 children, according to the U.S.

Centers for Disease Control and Prevention. But among military families, the rate is a startling 1 out of every 88 children, and in Silicon Valley the rate is roughly 1 in 77.

I want parents to see the urgent medical imperative to reduce their stress now.

Our current focus on our children and our schedules can leave us short of sleep, sex, and any sense of fun or belonging to a community. But we have convinced ourselves that we don't have time to relax with our spouses and socialize with our friends because our children's needs come first.

Contrary to popular belief, parents now spend more time with their kids than ever before, madly running from museum to concert to story time at the local library in a desperate—and stressed-out—effort to cram as much attention as possible into their time with their children.

But that's not what kids either want or need. Working parents guiltily assume their kids constantly hope for more family time. But when Dr. Ellen Galinsky, President and Co-Founder of the Families and Work Institute, surveyed more than 1,000 children, she was astonished by what they named as their greatest wish: "Kids were more likely to wish that their parents were less tired and less stressed," Dr. Galinsky found.

My book will give parents a "doctor's note" to relax, socialize more with other adults, and have more fun.

While parental stress is not the sole cause of today's epidemic of child ailments, it is one of several causes. Whereas parental stress does not always and inevitably lead to mental and physical disorders in children, it is a significant risk factor—and one that we can begin to fix right now. If reducing stress reduces the symptoms of even one child, we will have won a great victory.

This book's thesis may seem shocking, but it is surprising only because most of us are completely unaware of this parent-child mind-body connection. I will therefore lay out my arguments step-by-step, with compelling medical evidence and examples. I will then offer practical advice—you can think of it as preventive medicine—to keep good marriages from going bad, and to create a healthy space for our children.

I wish I could stamp every page of my book with the following reminder: "It's not about gender. It's not about blaming mothers." Rather, it's about the (insidiously) rising levels of stress in our society, and we need to wake up to the fact that our increasing isolation is causing our mounting stress levels—but it's our kids who pay the price.

We'll explore strategies that mothers, fathers, and couples can put into action to help reduce stress in their lives. The happy ending is that it's never too late to improve our families' health—to the benefit of our marriages and our children.

Good parenting is about building community and lowering stress. This book brings back the joy we used to feel in Sunday BBQs and extended-family get-togethers, in quiet time doing "nothing" with our children or with family meals. This can not only reduce the stress and anxiety that is crushing today's parents but can also produce children who are healthier both mentally and physically. We can rediscover a sense of cooperation and pride in doing good deeds to help others. We can raise our children to become citizens, rather than consumers. We can use preventive medicine to keep good marriages from going bad, so we will have a best friend to grow old with, and our children will grow up with a successful model for their own future marriages.

So yes, the news is dire, but there's a happy ending. Our healthy relationships are the best gift we can give our children.

- David Code, State College, PA

PART ONE

HOW A PARENT'S STRESS GETS UNDER A CHILD'S SKIN

Chapter 1

Today's Epidemic of Stress and Child Disorders

Today's parents of children under 18 are part of the Supposed-To Generation. We all want to do what's best for our children, but we are living in a time when we are supposed to do more and more, with less and less outside support from our families, community and friends. If you're a parent who helps your child with multiple activities—from soccer games and piano lessons to school plays, science fairs, and long nights of helping with homework, as well as planning your weekends around the ten things your children need to do—you are not alone. You are doing what the self-proclaimed experts and popular parenting books say you are supposed to do. But it may not be the right thing for your children.

What if our best intentions are having unintended side-effects, making it more likely that our children will develop ADHD, asthma, obesity or sensory disorders? What if our best intentions turn out to be the reason so many children suffer from frequent illnesses, food allergies, learning disabilities, or Oppositional Defiant Disorder (ODD)? These problems seem so different that they couldn't possibly be connected.

Except that maybe they are. Even small amounts of parental stress have been linked to today's most common child disorders, from colic to asthma. For example:

- A 2005 German study found that, if women encountered conflict at work, financial difficulties, or marital problems during pregnancy, their newborns were much more likely to suffer from colic during the first 6 months of life. A 2007 Danish study of mothers who encountered psychosocial stress during their pregnancies showed that their newborns were over 3 times more likely to have colic;

- A 2007 study found that if a mother is stressed during pregnancy, her child is substantially more likely to develop emotional or cognitive problems, including an increased risk of ADHD, anxiety, and language delay—whether or not the mother experiences postnatal depression and anxiety;

- A 2008 Harvard study found that children of parents with high stress levels were more than twice as likely to develop asthma or allergies. The study's lead author, Rosalind Wright, states that "maternal stress such as that precipitated by financial problems or relationship issues…can be thought of as a social pollutant that, when 'breathed' into the body, may influence the body's immune response similar to the effects of physical pollutants."

- A 2009 Australian study of 5,800 mothers showed that children born of anxious mothers were 64% more likely to have asthma at age 7;

- A 2008 Harvard review of the research on parental stress showed that stress during pregnancy increased the risk for babies to develop learning deficits, temper tantrums, seizure disorders, high sensitivity to stimuli, autism, and immune disorders such as allergies and asthma. A 2009 British study agrees;

- A 2008 Australian study concluded that stressed parents who were socially isolated or dissatisfied with their partners tended to have children who displayed higher levels of aggression or oppositional defiance;

- A 2007 New Zealand study states that obesity in children has risen over 40% in the past 16 years, and lists prenatal stress as one factor. A 2010 Danish study of more than 65,000 children found that prenatal stress made a child 68% more likely to be overweight at age 12;
- A 2002 UCLA study showed that families characterized either by tension or else cold, distant relationships tended to produce children who went on to develop mental health disorders, major chronic diseases, and early mortality.

Being financially well-off does not protect parents from stress, nor their children from the ill effects of that stress. Stress affects all children, rich or poor. One study analyzed the health care records of almost 14,000 families to discover that, in high-income households, children of anxious mothers were 44% more likely to develop asthma than poorer families.

Many people believe child ailments are largely, if not wholly, genetic and therefore heritable, but research is showing that is not the case. Although there is a genetic component to many illnesses, from schizophrenia to cancer, that does not mean these complex disorders are passed down from parent to child like, say, eye color. The public's beliefs about genetics lag far behind recent scientific research.

For example, studies of nearly 6,000 British children in 2009 and of 3,000 California children in 2008 concluded that parental stress increases the risk of asthma in kids. The study's authors noted that children in highly-stressed families were almost three times more likely to develop asthma than children of non-stressed families.

The results were the same even when the parents had no history of asthma whatsoever.

Another study of 4,400 children in 2005 suggested that offspring of stressed parents are almost twice as likely to develop Type 1 diabetes, and the study's authors added that a family's stressful life events increased the children's diabetes risk by 230 percent.

This was true even for children with no parental history of the disease.

Studies of twins are considered the gold standard for determining which disorders are genetically inherited, and which are not. A 2011 Stanford twin study found that, even among identical twins with the same genetic material, in only 60% of cases did both twins develop autism. The Stanford researchers concluded that genetics plays a much smaller role in developing autism than is widely assumed.

The list goes on, with medical studies showing that the children of stressed parents get sick more often, and suffer from more chronic health problems. Unfortunately, many parents don't recognize how stressed their lives have become.

What is Stress?

What people call stress can be a lot of different things, both inside our minds, and outside our bodies. There are outside stressors in our relationships, home or workplace, but there is also an inner, emotional response to these pressures (for example, anxious or depressed feelings) inside our minds.

Some people think of stress as an external force, over which they have limited control. For example, the inevitable hassles of daily life, such as job deadlines or a baby screaming with an ear infection, are stressful. We may exert some control over these stressors by taking on fewer responsibilities, or by reminding ourselves to "keep things in perspective." But there are also stressors over which we have less control, such as being born into poverty, or traumatic events like natural disasters or war-related experiences.

Regardless of how we define the many kinds of stress, the common denominator is the physical response that takes place in our bodies, starting in the brain, known as the *stress response*. It is an instinctive response that we share with many animals, which evolved to help us anticipate and respond to danger. Let me explain:

In the human brain, one key component in the stress response begins in the *hypothalamic-pituitary-adrenal (HPA) axis*, which is like a command-and-control center in the brain; it constantly monitors our environment for threats to our security. When a threat triggers our stress response, the brain sounds the alarm throughout our nervous system and dumps stress hormones (e.g., adrenalin, steroids) into our bloodstream. These stress hormones alert the body to put the digestive, immune, and other systems on hold in order to muster the body's resources toward more immediate needs, such as the *fight-or-flight* reaction.

However, an overreactive stress response can result in illness. Stress that is extreme (e.g., surviving an earthquake) or more chronic (e.g., money worries or relationship problems that go on for weeks or months) may adversely affect our stress response. Our stress response is meant to switch-on only for acute or immediate danger, but too much stress can cause it to instead remain switched-on constantly. At the very least, a constantly switched-on stress response makes us feel irritable or anxious. But over time it can also cause problems with our digestion, sleep patterns, memory, immunity, blood pressure, and many other bodily systems.

Scientists can objectively measure how fired-up our stress response is by testing how many stress hormones are in our blood or saliva. This gives researchers an objective picture of how active our stress response is at a given moment, regardless of whatever feelings we may report.

We may feel any feeling on the spectrum from mild, temporary anxiety to chronic, rampant stress, but the HPA axis of our brain is based on a very primal, instinctive response, that goes something like this: Small threat? Send a few stress hormones. Big threat? Send many stress hormones. Lingering threat? Keep stress hormones circulating, just in case, so the body remains chronically on high alert. For example:

1)   We might feel mildly anxious or worried about a job interview, and our stress hormone count rises briefly above our normal, baseline score;

2)   We might leave the house after an argument with our spouses, and though we smile sweetly to our neighbor as though we're feeling happy, the stress hormone counts in our bloodstream would tell otherwise;

3)   A parent with tense relationships among spouse, family, or in-laws might also have a stress response on chronic high-alert. The parent might insist, "I'm fine!" but his or her stress hormone levels would be high, making the parent more irritable;

4) A mentally ill person might have a stress response that remains chronically on high-alert, seldom returning to baseline levels, so he or she often feels anxious or high-strung.

So, what is stress? For the purposes of this book, stress is the number of stress hormones coursing through our veins—a quantifiable physiological response that exists whether we are aware of our stress or not. And the level of stress hormones in our blood has an impact on our health, as well as the health of our children—both in the womb, and after they are born. Here's how:

Stress During Pregnancy Affects the Fetus

Science has recently made great strides in understanding how stress impacts a child's development—not only in the child's early years, but even while the child is still in the womb. Just like alcohol and nicotine, stress hormones cross the placenta and cause damage to the developing brain cells of the fetus, as we will discuss in Chapter 2. Dr. Dennis Kinney, director of the Genetics Laboratory at Harvard Medical School, writes:

> It is noteworthy [ ] that many different studies with humans have found significant associations between behavioral problems and prenatal exposure to more common life events or to reports of maternal anxiety. In these studies, the measures of maternal stress are more representative of the kinds of stresses to which children are likely to be exposed prenatally.

In other words, many scientific studies conclude that even a mother's stress from normal, everyday hassles during her pregnancy has been linked to behavioral problems in children. Among the sources of stress:

- working with a difficult boss;
- a career change;
- moving to a new community;
- ongoing tension with a parent or relative;
- a marriage that has grown quarrelsome or distant; and
- even a severe storm.

Stress affects the genes of a child. These kinds of alterations in genes are called *epigenetic* changes. Unlike the better-known changes called mutations, epigenetic changes do not alter the underlying genetic code, but they do affect whether or not a gene has its programmed effect, for good or ill. In Chapter 4 I will discuss recent breakthroughs in the science of epigenetics and how this new field can help us understand the epidemic of childhood illnesses. But first, here's a preview:

A Breakthrough in the Science of Genetics

Many people assume that today's epidemic in children's mental and physical health is mainly genetic in origin, but few people are aware that a new chapter has been written in the debate of Nature vs. Nurture, and it's a game-changer. It turns out that Nature—our genes—are not as set-in-stone and unchanging as we thought. And Nurture—our family environment—has a greater influence than we ever imagined, even as a child develops in the womb.

Scientists have discovered a kind of "on-off switch" on our genes, called the *epigenome*. An important new branch of genetics called *epigenetics* reveals that some genes we inherit from our parents can be switched on or off by stress. This helps to explain why some children with a genetic predisposition to a disease develop symptoms, while others do not. Some "bad" genes might lie dormant forever, posing no risk, or they could be activated just like you turn on a light switch, with negative consequences for physical and mental health. Similarly, "good" genes can be expressed, giving us their benefit, or they can be switched-off, denying us their benefit.

The shocking news is that the more stress a child picks up from a parent, the greater the risk that the child will develop full-blown symptoms. To describe this process in terms of Nature vs. Nurture, if the nurture is stressful, the nature of genes can be affected a lot more than we thought.

How Kids Pick Up on Everything

Children are like little sponges, soaking up the free-floating stress in today's anxious households until their developing nervous systems hit "overload," at which point they act-out, or develop symptoms of mental or physical illness. Parents already knew that kids pick up on everything, but scientists have recently learned how: *attunement*—the subject of Chapter 3.

This new research on parental stress is crucial to every family, because the mind-body connection is a factor in almost every child's behavior. We tend to think of the mind-body connection in terms of our own mind affecting our own body—for example, our own stress weakens our immune system so we are more likely to catch cold. But science has discovered how a parent's mind affects a child's body, through a kind of "emotional pipeline" between parent and child, known as *attunement*.

Attunement is basically a fancy word for what we used to call the mother-infant bond, where parent and child are so attuned to each other that the child can pick up on a parent's stress and absorb it almost by osmosis. As a result, parental stress can weaken the development of a child's brain or immune system, increasing the risk of allergies, obesity, or mental disorders.

Briefly: from birth, a child possesses an exquisite sensitivity to a caregiver's tone of voice, facial expressions, eye movement, body language, and mood. We might call this the mother-infant bond, but neuroscientists call it *attunement*, a kind of "emotional pipeline" of communication, where caregiver and infant are tuned-in to each other.

One possible mechanism for this attunement may be their brains' mirror neurons, which allow them to reflect the emotions they sense the other is feeling. Mirror neurons appear to be what gives humans our capacity for empathy, but they also make children so sensitive to their parents' moods that kids can catch a parent's emotions just like they catch a virus. So, stress is highly contagious between parent and child, even if the parent is unaware of his or her own anxiety.

Let me underline that word, *unaware*. Many of today's parents may not realize just how high their stress levels have become. It requires patience and an open mind to really look at our own stress levels honestly. Humans are funny creatures: we are often experts at finding fault in others, and we can tell if another person is living in denial. Yet sometimes stress (and our denial that we are stressed) is extremely difficult to spot in ourselves. The challenge is to examine whether we might be deluding ourselves about the levels of stress in our lives. This book is meant to help bring those uncomfortable aspects into our awareness.

Humans are Social Animals: Our Growing Isolation is Increasing our Stress

Why do our children seem to have more problems today than even during the Great Depression? Dr. Jean Twenge, of San Diego University, used the authoritative personality survey, the MMPI (Minnesota Multiphasic Personality Inventory) to compare today's youth with the responses of young people in the 1930's. She found that more than five times as many of today's high school and college students are dealing with anxiety and other mental health issues as did the youth of the Great Depression era. Dr. Twenge believes this is probably a conservative estimate, since many of today's young people are on medications that alleviate the symptoms the survey asks about.

It turns out we were so busy killing ourselves to make our kids happy that our stress is now making them unhealthy. Where did we go wrong?

We have forgotten that humans are social animals. Our primate cousins all groom each other because they instinctively know that socializing maintains the group cohesion and cooperation they need to survive. But Americans think socializing is optional, so we neglect the "social grooming" that improves our health and reduces our stress levels.

Remember in the 1990s, when the media coined the term *cocooning* to describe a trend in which people were socializing less and retreating to their homes more? We never hear about it anymore, but that's not because cocooning went away. It simply became the norm. We spend less time in community because our flight-response gets triggered so often that it governs our behavior much more than we realize.

What Causes Stress: The Vicious Circle of Flight-Response and Isolation

What is our flight-response?

When we hear the phrase, "fight-or-flight," perhaps we think of two bears fighting, or a herd of gazelles fleeing. But remember that humans are animals too. For example, we all know what our fight-response looks like when we argue, but few of us realize what our flight-response looks like. Our flight-response is avoidance—distancing ourselves emotionally from others. It is the silent killer of relationships, and an invisible source of great stress.

Understanding the flight-response is crucial to you, because the flight-response is the key component of a vicious circle that is rapidly escalating the stress in our lives today. In a nutshell, the vicious circle looks like this:

Our increasing levels of stress make us more edgy and irritable. So, in our daily interactions, our fight-or-flight response is triggered more easily, and more often. Whether we fight more often, or flee more often, the result is the same: we end up increasingly isolated. But, because humans are social animals with herd instincts, when we become more isolated we also feel more uneasy and anxious. Unfortunately, this increased anxiety makes us more edgy and irritable, thus continuing a self-perpetuating circle of escalating stress and isolation.

The above vicious circle explains why our levels of stress today are much higher than previous generations. This is one of the most important concepts in this entire book, so we will return often to this primal, unconscious flight instinct that causes stress in our interactions with others.

As our lifestyles grow faster and more isolated, our increasing anxiety and irritability mean more stress hormones in our bloodstream, so today's parents spend much more time in flight-mode than before. In the old days, when we spent more time in community, people who argued would make an effort to reconcile because "this is a small town after all." Today, most people simply default to their flight-response, and avoid people they disagree with. As our flight-response triggers more often, our circle of friends and acquaintances is getting smaller and smaller. And in the past 20 years, we haven't noticed how isolated and stressed-out we have become. But as Dr. Jean Twenge writes:

> *Many social statistics point to a breakdown in social connectedness.*
> *The divorce rate has increased, the birth rate has dropped, people marry*
> *later in life, and many more people now live alone (11% in 1950,*
> *compared with 25% in 1997). In addition, Putnam (2000) found that*
> *Americans are now less likely to join community organizations and visit*

friends than they once were. Connectedness can also be measured by levels of trust (Fukuyama, 1999), and these levels have also declined (only 18.3% of high school seniors in 1992 agreed that you can usually trust people, compared with 34.5% in 1975; Smith, 1997).

Many researchers in various other institutes have come to the same conclusion that Americans' isolation is rapidly increasing as we lead a more transient lifestyle. Between 1985 and 2004, the number of people who said they had no one to confide in has tripled to 25 percent of the population.

We visit our parents less often, drift away from our relatives, move away from our friends, and distance ourselves emotionally from our spouses. We work longer hours with more responsibility and pressure than before, and we spend more time in front of our electronic screens. We have even convinced ourselves that socializing face-to-screen online is just as fulfilling as face-to-face. As a result, studies show that, while social media are on the upswing, civility and real-life social skills are declining rapidly. Americans go on 60 percent fewer picnics today and families eat dinner together 40 percent less often compared with 1965, and a recent survey found that more than two-thirds of parents now allow their children to text during family meals.

Americans are far more isolated than they were only two decades ago. Take the real-life example of "Bella," who lives with her husband and three kids in Los Angeles:

I just got back from my usual summer with my family/extended family (15+ people) in our farmhouse on a tiny island off the coast of Seattle—with only 1 bathroom! And the prime emotion I feel is intense loneliness. I think people assume that I go to a small island in the NW for peace and alone-time in the summer which couldn't be farther from the truth. On a small island, you HAVE to be part of the community—everyone knows me and my family and my kids so there is very little privacy. In comparison, in Los Angeles, I can be totally alone, all day long, every day, unless I and my friends reach out to one another. And sometimes we forget that!

How Socializing Reduces our Stress

Dan Buettner, a *New York Times* best-selling author and former NPR reporter, studies what brings happiness in many cultures around the world, concluding that Americans underestimate the power of relationships to reduce stress and increase happiness, both in the community and the workplace:

> *...the happiest people in America socialize about seven hours a day... you're three times more likely to be happy if you are married ... and each new friend will boost your happiness about 10 percent...the biggest determinant of whether or not you'll like your job is if you have a best friend there, more so than how much you're paid, so proactively make sure you have good friends there. One way I assert doing that is: Be the one who organizes happy hour.*

People's happiness quotient is very high in Singapore, for instance, where people also spend a lot of time socializing with their parents:

> *[There are] tax laws in place that encourage people to stay closer to their aging parents. That way the elderly are taken care of and happier, and it turns out the way socialization works, we get more satisfaction retroactively by socializing with our parents than anybody else.*

Many of us have heard of the old Biblical commandment to "Honor thy father and thy mother..." but few of us know the second half of that sentence goes on to explain *why*: "...so that your days may be long and that it may go well with you..." Buettner's research may confirm the wisdom of this Old Testament commandment. Of course, some parental relationships may be so toxic that one needs professional help to achieve some kind of reconciliation. However, simply avoiding difficult relationships with one's parents creates unseen stress in both that child and, as I will explain in Chapter 6, her future offspring. In other words, some relationships may be stressful, but the alternative—isolation—is actually more so.

The goal of today's parent should be to socialize more, in order to reduce the anxiety in the household, so kids will absorb less stress. It may sound strange, but the shortest route to healthier kids is for parents to calm down, mellow out, and de-stress. The more Americans return to spending time with friends and relatives, the happier and healthier both parents and children will be.

The Mother Is Not to Blame

At first glance, this book may seem like a guilt-trip on parents, blaming them for every ailment their child develops. However, we cannot hold parents responsible for their increasing flight-response and the growing isolation and stress that results, because parents are not even aware of this.

Nor can we hold a woman responsible for the stress she feels during her pregnancy when so many sources of angst and anxiety are beyond her control. Rather, new research focuses on the impact of her circle of relationships.

Every baby develops within a mother who lives within a web of family relationships. The more stressful those relationships, the more common her flight-response, and the greater her isolation—therefore, the more stress hormones there are in her womb. But this mind-body connection also continues in a different form long after the child is born into the family environment where mother, father, and even close family members all contribute to the stress levels in the home.

So, how do we begin to tackle parents' stress levels? Let's start by pinpointing one of the biggest causes of stress in a mother—namely, her relationship with her husband. Researchers at McGill University in Canada recently found that, among women who test as anxious following the birth of a child, a big source of stress is an unsatisfactory marriage. The experts describe three ways in which stress levels in a family actually hinge on the marital relationship:

1) The support of a social network is key to mental health, so an unstable marriage full of arguments or the "Silent Treatment" can be a very anxiety-producing problem in the social support of the caregiver;

2) The quality of the marital relationship often determines how much the father is present in the household. If the relationship is troubled, he may withdraw emotionally, or even physically, from his marriage and perhaps from his offspring as well. Examples include a spouse who prefers to talk about home repair rather than sharing his feelings, or a spouse who works long hours, or has an affair;

3) The spouses' ability to control their emotions and their ability to resolve conflict become a model for the child's own future relationships in adulthood. For example, how quickly can a couple move from a shouting argument to, "So…what should we make for dinner tonight?"

What we do in our marriages today will have a lasting impact on our child's health and emotional well-being. It's a pretty heavy responsibility, but there are so many things we can do to improve the outlook for our children's future—and many solutions begin with simple changes that are fun for parents.

Your Marriage Affects Your Child More Than You Think

It's obvious that marital conflict is stressful, but people seldom realize that distancing emotionally from one's spouse also leaves one more isolated and stressed. On the surface, the flight-response may seem more peaceful than the fight-response, but the level of stress hormones produced in the brain is the same, whether one is in fight-mode or flight-mode.

Contrary to popular belief, the biggest source of stress in our lives is not our jobs. Sure, our workload and deadlines are stressful, but the real stressor at work is when we're not getting along with our boss or a colleague. Relationships are our biggest source of stress, whether in the boardroom, the bedroom, or the dinner table at Thanksgiving.

The more tension we have in our relationships, the more time we spend in fight-or-flight mode, with stress hormones coursing through our bloodstream. Therefore, mothers with good relationships feel less stress and pass fewer stress hormones through their placenta, so their babies' brains and immune systems can develop in a healthier environment.

Dr. Vivette Glover, a stress expert at London's Imperial College, underlines how relationships are the main source of anxiety for mothers with stressful pregnancies: "We want fathers …to see how they can help with the development of their child even before the birth, by helping their partner to stay happy." Her statement is based on a study suggesting that when mothers experienced marital discord, when they separated or divorced during pregnancy, or if they were cruelly treated by their partners, it had a great impact on the fetus, making it more likely that the child would develop behavior problems and experience neurodevelopmental delays.

In this book, I will explain the very real-world, debilitating effects of ignoring the stress in relationships and households. In plain language, I will explain how you as a parent can make changes that will transform your own life and make a significant difference in the lives of your children, whether they have behavioral issues or allergies.

If you find your stress level beginning to rise as you read of how parental stress harms children, don't worry—the irony is not lost on me. The conversation in your head might be something like, "Yikes! I'm hurting my kids! Reading this book is stressing me out because I'm worried about the harm already done!"

Take comfort in the fact that you simply didn't know. But what we don't know can indeed hurt us, and it's in our children's best interest that we confront the truth. The good news is, the effects of our stress are reversible, so let's start by learning everything we can, and we'll address solutions in Part 3 of this book.

And Now, the Happy Ending

Knowledge is power, and the solution to this problem of child disorders is not only a relief—it's actually fun! Who wouldn't want to socialize more if their doctor prescribed it?

The empowering message of this research is that parents (or expecting parents) can reduce or even prevent some symptoms of disorders in their child by tamping-down the anxiety levels in their marriage.

There are significant changes and strategies that can help you create a healthy environment for your child regardless of where he or she falls on the spectrum—from minor acting-out behaviors right on down the line to serious health issues. Whether you are an expecting parent or a long-established family, this book will give you practical tools that you can put into action today.

You may have an emotional reaction to some of this book's conclusions and the advice offered. Remind yourself that this is not a blame game. The goal is to arm yourself with knowledge that can help you create a better, healthier life for yourself, your spouse and your children. Not every scenario will apply to you—there is no one-size fits all approach.

Let me be very clear: this news of how your mind connects to your child's body is like getting ten vaccinations at once—it stings at first, but then your whole family is protected for years to come. What may seem like a bitter pill to swallow can actually bring tremendous relief and empowerment to overwhelmed parents. Things suddenly begin to "make sense." This relief, and a new, clear strategy to improve their child's health, can transcend blame and fill parents with hope.

In other words, this story has a very happy ending, but you have to slay the dragon first. Real-life stories of parents (including myself!) who are going through the same challenges will show you that you are not alone.

You may be relieved to know that we are not aiming at perfection. Your only goal should be to *make progress*.

Imagine for a moment that you could somehow compare your family to other families on a graph, charting each family on a "Scale of Stress." It doesn't matter if you start out at 10 points lower than your neighbor's family on the Scale of Stress, or 20 points higher. What matters is to begin wherever you are at on the Scale of Stress, and to simply improve, say, 5 to 10 percent on the continuum. That's the ticket to a brighter future for our kids.

If parents avoid stress during pregnancy and socialize more with their spouses, family and friends, they greatly increase the odds that their children will be born with calmer, healthier brains and immune systems. In other words, the more we scratch our primal itch to socialize with friends and family members, the lower our stress, and the healthier our kids.

So, knowledge is power. And once we realize how we may be

creating a toxic, stressful environment for our kids, we can increase our social grooming to reduce our stress, which improves our family life and passes less baggage onto our kids. That's win-win for everyone.

When one examines the accumulated evidence, the parents of highly-stressed kids have certain characteristics that appear again and again. One might say there seems to be a typical pattern of behaviors by which parental stress can become a child's ailment. It's like a mind-body connection between parent and child—a parent's anxious mind affects a child's sensitive body.

It is very important to recognize these typical behaviors in parents, because once understood, this same pattern can be seen in most families, whether mildly- or greatly-stressed. It is easier to learn how to see this pattern in highly-stressed families first, and then it can be detected in less anxious families. So, let's start by looking at a few experiences at the extreme end of the spectrum. Although your family may not be facing the same situation, it's easier to spot the pattern of how stress affects our genes if we look at an extreme case first.

Chapter 2

How Kids Pick Up On Everything,
Part 1—In the Womb

It is said that a Muslim man went to his Imam, seeking advice and saying, "O Wise One, our first child was born into our family yesterday. Please teach me how to raise him well."

"Born yesterday?" the Imam said, "You are nine months late."

One Mother's Story:

Victoria Francis-Lovings of Boston believes that her marital problems and isolation from her parents contributed to her child's ADHD:

> *My entire pregnancy was very stressful…I was financially strapped and my husband at the time had no desire of supporting me or the baby. My family wasn't speaking to me because I was a disappointment for dropping out of school [pregnant]. It was an incredibly stressful time for me and my baby.*

Of course, no one would suggest that Victoria's marital stress was the sole cause of her son's ADHD. But might it have been a risk factor?

One Doctor's Story:

At George Washington University in Washington, D.C., Dr. Valerie Hu studies pregnant women under stress to measure its impact on children's health. When asked what led her to this research, she replied, "I have a 23-year-old autistic son. There was no history of mental illness genes in our family, so I always wondered what could have contributed to my son's autism."

Dr. Hu remembers, "When I was pregnant with my son, I was under a lot of stress at work, because I had a horrible boss. I think I handled it pretty well, but who knows what my body was doing under that pressure…"

Dr. Hu noticed an increasing number of medical studies linking parental stress to children with mental or physical problems. She gives seminars to families of autistic kids across the country, and she often tells her story about the possible role of her high stress during her own pregnancy. She says parents often nod knowingly as they listen to her, because they are relieved to be hearing a theory that finally makes sense to them, instead of blaming vaccines or genetics when there is no history of mental illness in their families.

Did the stress Victoria and Dr. Hu experienced in their pregnancies somehow contribute to their children's disorders? It's a question worth asking, because new research suggests that the stress level of parents is a major risk factor in children's health, from colic and minor learning disabilities to major illnesses such as autism, asthma and diabetes.

Such assertions may seem shocking, but the evidence is mounting. The National Scientific Council on the Developing Child at Harvard University is one of the world's premier research institutes focusing on child neurodevelopment, bringing together experts from such top medical schools as Harvard, Yale, Columbia, Stanford, Georgetown, and the University of Southern California. The Council is quite clear about the implications of parental stress on child development:

The realization that stresses experienced by parents and other caregivers can affect a child's developing brain architecture and chemistry in a way that makes some children more susceptible to stress-related disorders later in life is startling news to most people.

This chapter aims to dispel two popular myths:

- Myth #1: <u>The first few years of a child's life are the key developmental years</u>. In fact, the nine months of pregnancy have more impact on a child's personality and health, although the first few years are important, too;
- Myth #2: <u>A child's mental or physical problems are due to bad luck, bad genes, or both</u>. In fact, stress hormones cross the placenta, and stress has been linked to developmental problems in the fetus. This is actually great news, because you now have a medical reason to kick back, relax, and have fun during your pregnancy.

This chapter describes how the parents' stress affects the health of their child prenatally, and Chapter 3 explains how kids are still sensitive to stress after they are born. The good news comes in Chapter 4, when we will discuss how parents have the power to *change* the story of our children's health. But first, we need to understand the details of how stress can impact the health of our children, even in the womb, in a process known as *Prenatal Programming*.

A pregnant woman's stress hormones can cross her placenta, just as alcohol or nicotine do. Too many stress hormones in the womb affect the neurodevelopment of the fetus. Understanding prenatal programming, and how it impacts your child for a lifetime, is the first step in learning how to influence it for the better.

Stress Hormones Cross the Placenta: Prenatal Programming

After working with many families in crisis as an Episcopal minister, I wanted to offer parents some preventive medicine, so I wrote my first book, *To Raise Happy Kids, Put Your Marriage First*, which advised families how to prevent the kind of crises I observed so often. I knew my advice had struck a chord when my book became a sell-out success first in England and then in Canada. But even as the *Wall Street Journal* and the *New York Times* published articles on my work, I was already looking for a better way to help more families prevent the kind of problems that have become epidemic in our society.

Although I started out looking for solutions to children's behavioral problems, I ended up finding more and more evidence of a worrisome pattern in children's mental and physical health. For example, in doing research for that book, I was shocked to discover more than 100 scientific and medical articles linking parental stress to children's health, with many of the studies noting that stress hormones can cross the placenta. Too many stress hormones in the womb appear to affect the brain of the developing fetus, contributing to the frazzled neural synapses of ADHD and autism, or the overreactive immune system of asthma and diabetes. This may well be the mechanism by which maternal depression affects the fetus, as Harvard's National Scientific Council explains:

> *Maternal depression may begin to affect brain development in the fetus before birth. Depressed women produce higher levels of stress chemicals during pregnancy, which reduce fetal growth and are associated with an increased risk for premature labor. Depressive symptoms in an expectant mother also have been shown to be associated with altered immune functioning in her baby after birth. Even more striking, recent research has found that prenatal depression can be linked to the silencing of a gene that controls the over-production of stress chemicals. Thus, by the time of birth, the infant of a seriously depressed mother may have sustained effects on his or her stress response and immune systems. (Paper 8, Pg 4)*

This research may seem to suggest that the mother is directly responsible for her child's health. In fact, the studies show just the opposite. The reason a mother is not to blame is that her main source of stress is not in her mind, but rather in her relationships—especially with her husband and parents. It takes two to tango. New research suggests that it is largely the quality of our relationships that determines how much stress we feel, as Harvard's National Scientific Council continues:

> For example, mothers experiencing depression are often also young, socially isolated, economically or educationally disadvantaged, and burdened by more family conflict and stressful life events than mothers who are not depressed. (Paper 8, Pg 4)

In Chapter 6, we will examine how much of our stress stems from our relationships. We will also look at the vicious circle of our increasing flight-response, and the resulting isolation and stress which in turn triggers the flight-response more often. But for now, let's take a look at the causes and consequences of prenatal stress.

Ancient Greek, Chinese and Indian Cultures Knew About Prenatal Stress

Dr. Nicole Talge, now a researcher at Michigan State University Department of Epidemiology, still remembers clearly when she was six years old and her sister was born. She wondered what kind of person the new arrival would become: What will her personality be like? What will she like to do?

Dr. Talge says she also was very touched by stories of young children facing adversity, and she knew that ideally, she would choose a profession that would allow her to promote children's health and well-being. "I thought I would become a medical doctor," she says, "but my squeamishness (and fainting!) around blood put an end to that aspiration by the time I was a high-schooler. In the end, I felt that pursuing a research career might still allow me to make a difference in child health, while at the same time, minimizing my contact with blood!"

In her review of the research literature on the impact of prenatal stress, she found that, if a mother is emotionally stressed during her pregnancy, her baby is much more likely to develop ADHD, learning disabilities or anxiety problems.

As long ago as 400 B.C., Hippocrates wrote about how a woman's emotions influence the outcome of her pregnancy. The same concept is echoed in the ancient Hindu epic, *The Mahabharata*: "The daughter of Virata . . . [was] exceedingly afflicted by grief on account of the death of her husband . . . They all feared that the embryo in her womb might be destroyed." (Book 14, Section LXII). And the Chinese, who believed in the importance of a mother's emotions during pregnancy, created what was arguably the first prenatal clinic over a thousand years ago, focusing as much on emotional health as physical health.

Most people know that smoking or drinking can harm the fetus, because nicotine and alcohol can pass through the placenta to a child in utero. But parents may not realize that a mother's stress hormones can also pass through the placenta.

When we describe a rush of adrenaline during a time of excitement or fear, we are describing our body's stress response. Basically, our stress response triggers a rush of adrenaline, cortisol and other stress hormones, which increases our strength or reaction times, so we can fight better or flee faster.

Generally speaking, the higher the mother's stress hormone levels, the higher the stress hormone levels in her fetus. This is likely an evolutionary legacy: in our caveman days, extra stress hormones during pregnancy would have been a survival mechanism. Those extra stress hormones would render a mother hypersensitive, extra-vigilant, and therefore safer. Perhaps Mother Nature allowed the mother's extra stress hormones to cross the placenta in order to "program" the fetus to be prepared for a dangerous environment, full of predators, into which he or she was being born.

Unfortunately, this tendency to overreact has probably outlived its usefulness. The stress response evolved in a world very different from today's, when the greatest risk is not being unable to outrun a saber-toothed tiger (a task for which a brief surge of adrenaline pumping through your arteries would be quite useful) but insane drivers, final exams, tax audits, and terrorist alerts. The persistently-elevated levels of stress hormones caused by these chronic, low-level stressors, unfortunately, causes more harm than good.

Indeed, the hypersensitivity which served our ancestors well may now have begun to lead to neurodevelopmental disorders. It is important to remember that stress, anxiety, and depression have at least one factor in common: they lead to an overreactive stress-response in the brain.

One British doctor has dedicated her career to studying the stress response in pregnant women, and its impact on their children.

Both Dr. Vivette Glover and her husband Jonathan have made great contributions to medicine: he for his studies on bioethics, and she for her research at Imperial College in London on prenatal stress—in particular its effects on fetal development.

Dr. Glover's research suggests that if a pregnant woman is under stress, her bloodstream carries many stress hormones, which may cross the placenta into the amniotic fluid. Too many stress hormones appear to have a negative effect on the development of the fetal brain's stress-response. In other words, if the fetal brain is forming in a "bath of stress hormones," it may program the fetus to create an over-sensitive, overreactive stress-response. As Dr. Glover writes, "The evidence for an association between maternal stress, depression or anxiety in pregnancy and an adverse neurodevelopmental outcome for the child is now substantial."

Researchers from Around the World Agree on Effects of Prenatal Stress

Dr. Glover's research on British families has been duplicated by experts in countries around the world, including the United States, Britain, Belgium, Canada and Australia:

Dr. Catherine Monk, a professor of clinical psychology at Columbia University Medical Center in New York, monitored the heart rate, blood pressure, and nervous-system arousal of pregnant women who were anxious and depressed, and also measured the movements and heart rates of their fetuses. She then compared them to a group of pregnant women with normal moods: the fetuses of anxious or depressed women had a much higher rate of disturbances *in utero*.

In 2010, Dr. Monk published a review of the scientific literature on prenatal stress, and concluded that it affects fetal development and a child's mental health across the entire lifespan. She points out the irony that gestational diabetes is much less common than depression during pregnancy, and yet mothers are routinely screened for diabetes but not for depression, which appears to affect the health of more babies. Dr. Monk therefore strongly argues for mental health testing during pregnancy as a way to reduce the impact of mood disorders on future generations.

A review of the scientific literature by Drs. Eric Taylor and Jody Warner Rogers of King's College Department of Psychiatry in London, shows that stress, both *in utero* and postnatally, has been linked to learning disabilities, ADHD, and autism. In Belgium, a study of 71 mothers by Dr. Bea Van den Bergh of Catholic University of Leuven found that a child's risk of developing ADHD was 22 percent higher if the mother was anxious during pregnancy than if she was not.

In Canada, a study of 203 children led by Dr. Natalie Grizneko of the Department of Psychiatry at McGill University in Montreal concluded that babies who were exposed to moderate or severe prenatal stress tended to develop more severe symptoms of ADHD. She, too, emphasized the importance of reducing stress in pregnant women.

Dr. Curt Sandman of the University of California, Irvine did a review of the research supporting a non-genetic basis for autism. For example, he cites experiments where researchers studied fetuses who were conceived by in vitro fertilization, from eggs that had no genetic relationship to the host mother. Those fetuses which were exposed to stress in utero went on to suffer neurodevelopmental effects. That suggests that inherited genes are not the primary factor in play here, a cautionary note for anyone who still believes genetics are the primary cause of disorders.

Researchers around the world have come to the same conclusion: a mother's stress during pregnancy affects the neurodevelopment of the fetus. Perhaps the most impressive evidence comes from a geneticist at Harvard.

Harvard's Dennis Kinney Revolutionizes Stress Research

As director of the Genetics Laboratory at Harvard's McLean Psychiatric Hospital, Dennis Kinney is a major player in autism research. McLean Hospital is famous for its long list of Nobel- and Pulitzer-prize winners—both doctors who work there and patients who have been treated there. McLean also houses the largest private neuroscientific research program in the world, with funding from prominent groups such as Autism Speaks and the National Institute of Health.

Dr. Kinney's discoveries began with his analysis of the studies of twins with autism. Twin studies have always been considered the gold standard for genetic research, because until recently they were the best way to determine whether or not an illness is genetic. This is because identical twins develop from the same, single egg that has been fertilized by the same, single sperm, so they have identical genes. Therefore, if both identical twins develop autism, one could assume that autism must be a genetic disease, and that both twins apparently inherited "autism genes" from that single egg or sperm they shared at conception.

When Dr. Kinney examined four well-known twin studies of children with autism, his conclusions were initially as expected. In fraternal twins (that is, non-identical twins who are no more genetically related than any other siblings), the studies showed that if one twin had autism, the odds that the other twin also had autism were between 0 and 30%. This lack of concordance was to be expected, since each fraternal twin is developing from separate eggs, with separate DNA. But the data on identical twins, who have identical DNA, did not add up. If one identical twin had autism, the chances of the other having autism were between 36 percent and 96 percent. This was surprising, because if autism were a genetic disease, then one would expect 100 percent of identical twins to share the "autism gene" they inherited at conception. Since identical twins have identical genes, how could one explain the fact that in 64 percent of the cases in which one twin develops autism, the identical twin does not?

Dr. Kinney concluded that there must be something else involved. If autism were inherited genetically, we would expect 100 percent of identical genes to inherit the "autism gene" the way we inherit a gene for our eye color. He therefore figured that identical twins inherit the same genetic predisposition to autism, but something in the environment interacts with these genes to "switch-on" autism in some identical twins but leave it switched off in some of their co-twins.

As it turns out, other researchers had also discovered this disparity among identical twins with a supposedly "genetically inherited" disease. A review of ASD (Autism Spectrum Disorders) literature by Dr. Daria Grafodatskaya of Toronto's Hospital for Sick Children also found that genetics play some role in ASD, but it may be a much smaller role than people assume, and study results vary widely. For example, if one twin in a set of identical twins shows autistic symptoms, some studies say the odds are up to 90 percent that the other twin will also show symptoms while others give the odds at 70 percent, or even 30 percent. In addition, there is often a great disparity in the type and degree of autistic symptoms in identical twins, despite their identical genes.

If identical twins, with the exact same genes, could show such a wide disparity in symptoms, there must be some other factor that influences which kids developed autism and which did not. Dr. Kinney had read many studies suggesting that prenatal stress was an important risk factor for autism, but often said these studies were too small, often sampling fewer than 100 families. Some also relied on self-reports. That is, after a child was diagnosed with autism, the shocked mothers would look back on their pregnancies and be tempted to fish for something—anything—that might have contributed to the child's ASD. Since such self-reports can be subjective and even inaccurate, Dr. Kinney wanted to create a definitive study, with solid, objective data on thousands of families.

He found his definitive experiment in the strangest of places: tropical storms in Louisiana.

Louisiana, like all states, keeps birth records of every baby born in the state. And the state mental health system also keeps records of every child diagnosed with autism. So statisticians can compare the number of live births to the number of children diagnosed with autism. This can tell us what percentage of babies develop autism, where they were born, and when.

This is where it gets interesting: Dr. Kinney decided to compare these birth and autism statistics with data on hurricanes and tropical storms. He figured that, if stress is a risk factor for autism, and severe storms are pretty stressful events, then perhaps women who experienced a hurricane during their pregnancy might be more likely to give birth to a child who goes on to develop autism.

This is known as a *natural experiment*. Most experiments are conducted in clean, orderly laboratories because scientists need to be sure that all their tests are conducted under the same conditions—so they can compare apples-to-apples in their data. But it's hard to study prenatal stress in a laboratory; you can't sit 100 pregnant women on chairs for nine months in your lab, feed them the same food, and give them stressful events at the same time, in order to make sure they have been exposed to the same conditions. Also, one never knows if other factors affect the women's stress levels: maybe they live in poverty, or maybe there is a history of anxiety in their families.

But sometimes Mother Nature gives researchers a natural event that turns a big swath of the population into a giant experiment. The key to a natural experiment is that, if thousands of people are subject to the same event at the same time, then one can reliably compare apples-to-apples when you measure how they were affected by the event. The exciting thing about the statistics in Louisiana is that the storms hit everyone in a given area, in a random, arbitrary manner—whether they were rich or poor, calm or stressed, sick or healthy.

Like most scientists, when Dr. Kinney began his experiment he was playing a hunch. But little did he know that his study would become a historic contribution to science. There are at least five fascinating reasons why:

First, this natural experiment gave the Harvard researchers a huge sample of more than 55,000 pregnant women who were impacted by one of ten severe storms that took place during a fifteen-year period. Whether you carried a supposed "autism gene" in your DNA or not, the wind still blew and the rain still rained on you. And the storms affected so many pregnant women that the data were not likely to be undermined by statistical flukes. That made it easier to believe that any trends in the graphs reflected reality and not random chance. One could easily discern whether those women actually gave birth to more autistic children than did women whose pregnancies did not occur during a hurricane.

Second, there was no subjective self-reporting from the mothers. No one was asked to look back on her pregnancy and guess what factor might have contributed to her child's autism. Dr. Kinney simply collected the names of all children who were *in utero* during the Louisiana storms, and matched them to the names of children later diagnosed with autism in the area the storms hit. In other words, he and his team compared fifteen years of storm data, from 1980 to 1995, to fifteen years of babies born in that same period, along with fifteen years of babies later diagnosed with autism. No one asked these mothers for their subjective recollections about their pregnancies, or if autism ran in their family. So the data include only objective statistics.

Third, there was no *confirmatory bias* in the study. Confirmatory bias is a fancy scientific way of saying, "We find what we're looking for." It's human nature to notice things that confirm our beliefs about the world. When scientists spend thousands of hours and sometimes millions of dollars on an experiment, it almost goes without saying that they are hoping for interesting results. If that happens, and if their hunch (or, more formally, hypothesis) proves correct, it means more research funding and prestige. When scientists are collecting data that are not black-and-white, it's always tempting to interpret the "gray areas" in favor of one's hunch.

The beauty of the Louisiana storm experiment is that the data on thousands of children was gathered by government workers who had no agenda regarding stress or autism. It wasn't in their interest to exaggerate the number of autism cases—in fact, they had no inkling that the data they were gathering would one day be analyzed in the way Dr. Kinney did. They were simply recording weather statistics, or birth statistics, or mental health statistics, and never envisioned any interaction among the three. They didn't know, and probably wouldn't care, that years later their statistics might be used in a study of prenatal stress. That's why in a natural experiment the numbers speak for themselves.

And speak they did. Dr. Kinney chose the ten most severe Louisiana storms between 1980 and 1995. More than 320,000 babies were *in utero* when these ten storms struck. Thirteen out of every 10,000 "storm babies" surveyed was diagnosed with autism—compared to four of every 10,000 babies who were not in utero during storms. That means babies whose mothers had been subject to the Louisiana storms were *more than three times more likely* to be diagnosed with autism!

This leads us to the fourth reason Dr. Kinney's experiment was historic. He was amazed to find that, the more severe the storm in a given Louisiana parish, the more women gave birth to babies who went on to be diagnosed with autism. This suggests that the higher the mother's stress level, the more likely her stress hormones would affect the development of the fetus. Scientists call this a *dose-response:* the greater the dose, the greater the response.

In this case, dose-response means that, of the ten storms measured, the most severe was linked to the most autistic kids, and so on down to the least severe, which was associated with the fewest autistic kids. This suggests that it was indeed the stress caused by the storm that increased the incidence of autism.

Dose-response is a blue-ribbon indicator of an experiment's accuracy. Since the incidence of autistic children corresponded to the severity of the storm, one can safely conclude it was the storm impacting the babies, rather than some other invisible factor. This lent further credibility to this natural experiment.

Stress During the 5th or 6th Month of Pregnancy is 4 Times More Harmful

The fifth reason Dr. Kinney's experiment was historic was his discovery that prenatal stress affects the fetus differently at different times in the pregnancy. In other words, there were periods when a fetus was much more vulnerable to the harmful effects of prenatal stress. For example, if the storm struck during a woman's first four months of pregnancy, the number of fetuses who went on to develop autism was relatively low: between 2.93 and 4.77 babies out of 10,000. But if a storm struck during a woman's fifth or sixth month, the rate increased to 17.74 autistic babies out of 10,000. The effect of a storm during months seven or eight went way down to only 3.48 babies per 10,000, but a storm during months nine or ten produced another spike in autism, with almost 11 babies per 10,000 who would go on to be diagnosed.

This news was startling. Why would stress affect the fetus so much more during months five, six, and nine of a pregnancy? In fact, other studies suggest that a baby is more vulnerable to stress hormones in the fifth and sixth month of pregnancy, including ground-breaking research in 2005 by Dr. David Beversdorf, the Chair of the Interdisciplinary Neuroscience Program at University of Missouri Medical School.

Dr. Beversdorf graduated from Indiana University and completed his neurology residency at Dartmouth. He told me of a formative event that led to his interest in prenatal stress. Some time ago, a close friend of his was pregnant when her eldest child drowned in a tragic accident. When she later gave birth to a son, he went on to develop autism. "It influenced my career," Beversdorf said, "and made me really wonder how the mind worked. And then I wondered if that particular stress story was important."

A member of the International Society for Autism Research, Dr. Beversdorf was doing research at Ohio State University's Department of Neurology when he and his colleagues studied 188 families with autistic kids to find out whether there was a particularly high-risk window of time during gestation when the fetus might be more vulnerable to stress.

Beversdorf's team analyzed various stressors, including: the death of a spouse, divorce, death of a close relative, being fired from work, and a change in the health of a close family member. There was a clear peak period of vulnerability that showed up on researchers' time graphs. Prenatal stress between 21 and 32 weeks of gestation had the greatest impact on a fetus, with a pronounced peak from 25 to 28 weeks.

This is the same window of vulnerability that Dr. Kinney found in his Louisiana storm study. The window seems to coincide with the period of development of certain parts of the brain that appear damaged in MRI's of autistic children's brains. "The findings in this study lend some support for the hypothesis that prenatal stress-related changes in the brain are a potential etiologic [i.e., causative] factor in autism," Beversdorf and his colleagues wrote.

Dr. Kinney agrees. As he wrote in a 2008 review article, *Prenatal Stress and Risk for Autism*, "There are more than 100 experiments published in the scientific literature on the effects of prenatal stress in laboratory animals… prenatal stress does not need to be either chronic or extremely severe in order to have a significant effect on postnatal development."

In this chapter we have discussed two important issues: 1) Stress crosses the placenta to affect development of a fetus; and 2) Even small amounts of stress can have a big impact on fetal development if the stress occurs during particularly sensitive periods during pregnancy.

Now that we understand the impact stress can have on a child's body while in the womb, let's examine how a stress passes from parent to child after the child is born.

Chapter 3

How Kids Pick Up On Everything, Part 2—After a Child is Born

At a recent social gathering, a mother I'll call Gail thanked me for an insight about the mind-body connection that she gained from one of my marriage seminars. She said, "My son has asthma, and I realized that every time I heard him cough my anxiety would spike. It even got to the point where he was afraid to cough in front of me! Your seminar taught me how to focus on what was going on in my marriage when my son coughed. I began to notice that I overreacted to my son's cough the most when my husband and I were avoiding tough topics in our marriage, which caused our stress levels to spike and me to over-focus on my son. But whenever I calmed down about my son's cough, his symptoms seemed to improve! So, now I argue more with my husband, but my son is healthier. I don't mind making that trade-off!"

In Chapter 2, I discussed how a fetus picks up on everything while in the womb. It is relatively easy to visualize a mother's stress hormones crossing the placenta into the womb, and the developing brain of a fetus. But once a child has left the womb, how does parental stress enter a child's body?

How do babies "catch" their parents' stress?

Scientists have recently learned how: *attunement*, a powerful form of non-verbal communication between parents and children. Attunement appears to depend on *mirror neurons*, specialized cells in the brain that apparently allow us to mirror the emotions of the person in front of us. Mirror neurons apparently underlie empathy and our capacity to feel what others are feeling. We will address three essential points in this chapter:

- The mother-infant bond is a temporary attachment of a caregiver to her infant to ensure that the infant thrives;

- But it's not just a loving mother caring for her naïve, mindless baby. Attunement is a constant, complex, and significant *two-way* interaction between two intelligent beings; it is through attunement that kids pick up on everything, and parents pass on their stress to their kids;

- This pattern of attunement between parent and child affects the child's relationships for life, because attunement is what shapes the child's brain to read the emotions of everyone the child meets as he or she grows into adulthood.

The Mother-Infant Bond: Ensuring Her Infant Will Thrive

The survival of our species depends on parents' commitment to their offspring, so evolution programmed moms to feel an instinctive emotional and psychological bond to their infant.

The human version of the mother-infant bond strongly resembles that of our primate cousins. With pregnancy, a rush of hormones such as estrogen and progesterone prime maternal instincts. At birth, a cascade of prolactin and oxytocin takes over, motivating primate mothers to nurture, feed and protect their offspring until they are mature enough to begin to fend for themselves. From rats to monkeys, oxytocin lubricates the relationship between caregiver and offspring. In experiments when scientists have blocked the flow of oxytocin, caregivers of many species lose interest in their offspring and no longer make the usual overtures to their babies.

The mother-infant bond in humans is good news, because it

guarantees a child's survival. Our child becomes the center of our world, and our parenting hormones help us ignore the sleep deprivation, the stinky diapers, and the colic (ever been there?). For example, if a baby cries, it is thanks to the mother-infant bond that the caregiver can't bear to hear her child's suffering. It's almost as if she has an "empathy overload," in that her child's suffering elicits such discomfort in her that she cannot help but soothe and take care of that child's needs right away. Studies have shown the power of a mother's neurological response to the sound of her own child's cries.

We may nod at this familiar empathy a caregiver feels for her child, but it may not have occurred to us that this empathy is mutual. Anyone who has worked in a hospital's neonatal ward can tell you how, when one baby cries, other babies within earshot soon join in. How can it be that newborn babies already show empathy?

The answer may lie in *mirror neurons*. Research is still in its early stages, but these specialized cells in the brains of many animals, including humans, may be what allow us to instantly read and reflect back the feelings of our fellow humans. This gives humans the capacity for empathy—to feel what our neighbor is feeling.

From birth, a child possesses an exquisite sensitivity to a caregiver's tone of voice, facial expressions, eye movement, body language, and mood. A baby is highly tuned to his caregiver's voice and body language. Mother Nature has equipped him with the ability to charm his caregiver, be adorable, and otherwise build rapport in a myriad of delightful ways. But he doesn't do this for fun. Babies have an agenda.

We often think of a newborn baby as a "clean slate," with an undeveloped brain. But as we will see below, babies are born much smarter than we realize, and basically hit the ground running—cognitively, at least. Some neuroscientists and psychologists have studied the way a baby instinctively knows how to cry, gesture, and communicate his needs. In fact, the wired-in ability of offspring to elicit the care they need is common to most animal newborns, from birds to monkeys. A baby has been programmed to instinctively pursue his best interests: surviving and thriving. He does this by establishing a rapport with his caregiver, and this relationship is his best insurance that maternal care will continue as long as possible.

Attunement: A Two-Way Conversation Between Mother and Child

Scientists refer to this dance of rapport between mother and child as *attunement*, a kind of "emotional pipeline" of communication between parent and child, and it's one of the most important concepts you'll read about in this book. As the name implies, attunement means caregiver and child are "tuned in" to each other, so they can sense the emotions the other is feeling.

There are two key points to remember about attunement:

First, attunement is a highly-sensitive, two-way communication between mother and child. It's almost as if mother and infant can read each other's minds. Children truly do pick up on everything. From birth, a child possesses an exquisite sensitivity to a caregiver's tone of voice, facial expressions, eye movement, body language, and mood. We grown-ups tend to put a lot of value on the words we speak to each other. Children and infants can read all our other cues, which explains their uncanny ability to know what's *really* going on in a family.

Second, with attunement, the stakes are sky-high for the infant, because his survival depends on his communication with his mother, and attunement is his only way of knowing whether his survival needs will continue to be met. Through this communication pipeline, the child is constantly sending new bids for attention, and constantly receiving reassuring messages that his mother is there for him.

Psychiatrists at Cornell Medical School have used hours of videotape of mother-child interactions to study and analyze this subconscious "dance of rapport" between caregiver and child. If the infant were to verbalize his thoughts to his mother, it might sound like, "Do you want me?...Do you want me now?...Do you still want me now?...How 'bout now?..." and so on. Every time his caregiver responds to his bids, the infant is reassured that his lifeline is intact and his survival is not threatened.

Nothing is more important to an infant than maintaining his caregiver's commitment to him. That's why, even in the womb, infants make it their full-time job, 24/7, to monitor their caregiver's cues and remain constantly vigilant of her. *In utero*, a fetus can analyze the chemistry of a mother's amniotic fluid, and listens in on his mother's communication with other humans. After birth, babies know their mother's scent and are experts on even the most subtle glance, gesture or tone of voice. Darwin himself described how infants keep detailed "files" on their mothers, because the only reality a child knows is that the mother-infant bond is essential to his survival. The infant depends on it for his very life, and instinctively behaves so as to strengthen that connection.

The complex give-and-take of attunement has all the tacit understanding and subtle, unconscious communication of other human relationships. For example, a caregiver coos at her baby in response to his squeal. Such affirming messages are sent back-and-forth roughly once every minute, as the caregiver mimics and matches the baby's level of emotion, which reassures the infant of being connected with his caregiver.

In sum, the attunement that occurs with the mother-infant bond serves several purposes: it inspires the caregiver to care for her infant, it helps the child survive and thrive, and it creates an "emotional pipeline" between parent and child. Attunement is like a non-stop, wordless conversation between parent and child, an interaction by which our children learn by osmosis, soaking up everything around them.

What many people may not realize is that attunement follows us into adulthood. Our brains' patterns of relating, which we establish as babies with our mothers, becomes our pattern of relating and developing rapport as adults. In other words, attunement wires our brains to read and reflect the emotions of those we meet, especially in close relationships.

A Child's Attunement Sets the Pattern for How She Interacts as an Adult

John Cacioppo, a University of Chicago psychologist, conducted a large study of the impact of relationships on health. He concludes that our nervous systems are highly attuned to our loved ones—which means mirror neurons have their pros and cons.

On the *pro* side, mirror neurons originally evolved in the brain as the embodiment of the herd instinct, allowing anxiety to spread quickly and put the whole group on alert if one member sensed imminent danger. This mirroring of emotions is also the basis of our ability to feel empathy.

But the disadvantage of mirror neurons is that they render us super-sensitive to the vibe of those around us. Since offspring depend on their parents for protection, children are instinctively so attuned to their parents' moods that kids can "catch" emotions from parents just like they catch a virus. Stress is therefore highly contagious between parent and child, even if the parent is unaware of his or her own anxiety.

This invisible, contagious aspect of stress can be seen in a study led by Dr. A. Clavarino of Australia's University of Queensland, which followed almost 4,000 children born in Brisbane between 1981 and 1983. The scientists measured the mothers' anxiety levels when the kids were between 0 and 5 years of age, and then counted the number of these kids who displayed ADHD symptoms at age 5 and again at 14. Result: children with anxious mothers were more than five times more likely to have ADHD.

A 2002 review by Dr. Rena Repetti of the Department of Psychology at the University of California, Los Angeles, titled, "Risky Families: Family Social Environments and the Mental and Physical Health of Offspring," concluded that stress is contagious: marriages characterized by conflict or avoidance create stressful, risky environments for children, who are therefore prone to develop mental problems or physical illnesses.

A couple's conflict or emotional distancing is interpreted by the child as a threat to her security. The resulting stress can trigger mental disorders, or chronic diseases that show up much later in life. Thus, a child's environment, both pre-and postnatally, can impact his or her health across the entire life span.

In other words, stress is highly contagious, especially in intimate relationships like marriage or parenting.

To sum up this chapter, the mother-infant bond is not a one-way street. It produces two-way communication between two intelligent beings, based on attunement. This attunement in infants goes on to become our adult model for every future relationship we develop. Children's brains are wired during infancy to pick up on everything in their household, and this continues into adulthood.

This raises the next question: once children have picked up a parent's stress and mirrored that stress in their own brains, how does that stress affect their health?

In Chapter 4, we will examine how children's brains react to the stress they absorb from parents by releasing cascades of hormones that regulate everything from their heartbeat to their fight-or-flight response. In particular, stress can affect the parts of the brain responsible for:

- Social competence—leading to behavior disorders;
- Emotional processing—leading to neurodevelopmental disorders;
- Immune response—leading to allergies and asthma.

There is a process by which a child's stress hormones in her bloodstream physically interact with the genes in her brain, as I will describe in the next chapter.

Chapter 4

How Parental Stress Affects a Child's Body—
Epigenetics

In the past several years, genetic research has taken a dramatic turn. Until recently, scientists tried to discover genes that caused specific diseases such as colon cancer or autism. Instead they found that *many* diseases may arise from the same mechanism in each gene. This mechanism is called the *epigenome,* and it is the most important discovery you've never heard of, because in many ways the epigenome programs your health and the health of your child.

In this chapter, we'll cover three main points:

a. ***Epigenetics: The On-Off Switch on Genes***

How do stress hormones harm fetal development? Medical researchers have recently discovered the *epigenome,* a kind of on-off switch on each gene. In simple terms, the epigenome is that part of a gene which acts as a switch, deciding whether that gene will express itself or not. It does not affect the sequence of chemical "letters" that make up the strands of DNA; it only switches the DNA off, a process known as *methylation*. Stress hormones appear to switch some "good" genes off, and some "bad" genes on.

b. ***Epigenetics Affect Every Child's Development***

Understanding epigenetics is crucial to every parent, because epigenetics affect the development of every child—it's simply a matter of degree: the higher the stress levels in the parents, the higher the risk that good genes will be switched off, and bad genes will be switched on, either in the womb or after birth;

c. ***Happy Ending: Epigenetics is Reversible***

But there is a happy ending, because harmful epigenetics may be stopped, or even reversed. According to UCLA's Curt Sandman and other experts, if parents reduce their stress levels, either during pregnancy or during a child's early years, not only does this prevent further damage to genes, but some genes can actually undo their "switching" and heal.

The Medical Discovery of Epigenetics—The "On-Off Switch" on Genes

These days, physicians often tell me they feel overwhelmed by the number of children they see with mental and physical problems. The public continues to believe these ailments must be genetic, and that our genes are "set" and pre-determined. Most people think we inherit certain illnesses the way we inherit eye color—it's "all in the genes," and we have little control over our genetic endowment. But traditional genetics cannot account for the alarming increase in childhood ailments—an increase far greater than can be explained by better diagnosis on the part of physicians.

Scientists from around the world have been wondering about this increase in child ailments for years. Let's explore what their research and studies have uncovered, and dispel some of the preconceptions we have, as parents and as a society, in order to get a clear understanding of how stress impacts the physical and mental health of our children.

The public's perception of the role of genetics in these illnesses greatly lags behind medical research. Today's increase in childhood mental and physical illnesses is not just a question of genes, as if Nature trumps Nurture. It is a question of Nature *and* Nurture. A parent's level of stress has a huge impact on a child's genetic predisposition toward a disease. The goal of this book is to raise consciousness on just how much we can do as preventive medicine for our children's mental and physical health.

Since the human genome was sequenced in 2003, hundreds of research studies on thousands of patients have found that any given gene carries only a modest risk for a particular ailment. Indeed, Harvard and Duke geneticists reported in 2009 that "most of the genetic link to disease remains unexplained."

Whereas ailments like autism, ADHD, and asthma are unlikely to have any one, single cause, there is one issue that is gaining attention as a significant risk factor for these and other ailments. That factor is stress.

Few members of the public are aware of the recent, important scientific discovery that stress affects our genes. But as Harvard's National Scientific Council on the Developing Child states:

> *Contrary to popular belief, the genes inherited from one's parents do not set a child's future development in stone… [T]he [family] environment in which one develops, before and soon after birth, provides powerful experiences that chemically modify certain genes which, in turn, define how much and when they are expressed. Thus, while genetic factors exert potent influences, environmental factors have the ability to alter family inheritance. (Paper #10, Pg 4)*

The "chemical modification" of genes refers to the *epigenome*, a kind of "on-off switch" located on each gene. Until recently, most people thought that "genetics" meant some unlucky children inherited a "gene" for ADHD or autism, and that's why they developed the illness. The gene was supposedly "set in stone."

But it turns out it's not that simple. All animals, including the human animal, have many dormant genes in their DNA, and they only work if switched on. The discovery of epigenetics is a game-changer in the debate of

Nature vs. Nurture—it turns out that Nurture affects Nature much more than we ever imagined, even before a child is born. In other words, Nature—our DNA—is not as rigid and unchanging as we assumed. And Nurture—our family environment—has a greater influence than we thought, even in the womb. If I had to sum up this book in one phrase, I would say it's about genes and stress, not about traditional genetics.

In a recent review of the research literature on autism, Dr. Arturas Petronas, head of the Krembil Family Epigenetics Laboratory and a professor at University of Toronto, lists several reasons why autism cannot be simply a "genetic" disorder:

1) Many parents with no psychiatric history give birth to babies who develop autism;

2) In identical twins, many kids do not develop autism even when their twin does;

3) Autism is much less common in girls than boys; and

4) Both onset and symptoms vary widely among autistic children, unlike genetic diseases such as, for example, Down Syndrome.

So yes, our children can inherit a genetic predisposition toward certain diseases. But the amount of stress interacting with those genes is one of the factors determining whether a child develops full-blown symptoms or not. As Harvard's National Scientific Council states:

> *New scientific research shows that environmental influences can actually affect whether and how genes are expressed. Thus, the old ideas that genes are 'set in stone' or that they alone determine development have been disproven. In fact, scientists have discovered that early experiences can determine how genes are turned on and off and even whether some are expressed at all. Therefore, the experiences children have early in life— and the environments in which they have them—shape their developing brain architecture and strongly affect whether they grow up to be healthy, productive members of society (Paper #10, Pg 1).*

Genetic research today is no longer about whether your kid inherits a "bad gene." When it comes to a child's ailments, it's about which bad genes are "switched on" and which good genes are switched off. Hundreds of genes—some helpful, some harmful—are involved in ailments like autism. Geneticists have given up searching for one single, "bad" gene that causes autism, diabetes, and other ailments, according to Duke geneticist David Goldstein, and now believe that hundreds of different genes may be involved.

The good news from epigenetics is that we are no longer hostage to our genes. The empowering message of this new research is that, if we change our children's environment, we may be able to change the switching of their genes—at least to some degree. Parents can reduce or even prevent some symptoms in their child by tamping down the anxiety levels in their families. Again, from Harvard's National Scientific Council:

> Science tells us that the chemical signatures imprinted on our genes during fetal and infant development can have significant influences on brain architecture that last a lifetime. Stated simply, the discovery of the epigenome provides an explanation, at the molecular level, for why and how early positive and negative experiences can have lifelong impacts… [and] effective interventions can literally alter how children's genes work and, thereby, have long-lasting effects on their mental and physical health, learning, and behavior. In this respect, the epigenome is the crucial link between the external environments that shape our experiences and the genes that guide our development. (WP 10 Pg 1)

To simplify things a bit: the epigenome is where a parent's stress physically impacts the genes of a child. It is important to understand that parental stress affects a child both in the womb and postnatally. As we learned in Chapter 2, the mother's stress hormones pass through the placenta, into the amniotic fluid, and eventually into the blood of the fetus which flows through the developing brain.

When those stress hormones come in contact with the epigenetic on-off switch of, say, a gene that normally helps a child process what she sees and hears, and turns it off, the gene will stop producing cells that would help to process sight and sound.

Once a baby is born, a parent's stress is no longer transferred via the placenta, but rather by attunement and mirror neurons. When the child senses and mirrors the parent's stress, the child creates his or her own stress hormones, which then interact with epigenetic switches in brain tissue as described above.

Let's look at a real-life example. Julie Clark is a mother from Texas, whose ASD daughter Meredith can easily become over stimulated. Let's assume Meredith encountered too many stress hormones, either *in utero* or postnatally, and a useful gene got switched off, thus changing her impression of Disneyland:

> *[I remember] our trip to Disneyland, at the end of first grade. I wanted her to experience the electric light parade, which I had loved as a teen. Well, take a kid on the autism spectrum, who has sensory processing difficulties, out at night, in the dark, and expose them to all sorts of noises and lights. Guess what you get? An experience she remembers to this day. Not in a good way.*

> *I felt horrible, and still do. At the time, I thought she'd be OK once it got going, and kept trying to reassure her and make her sit through it, which was a mistake. I totally underestimated the negative effect it would have on her sensory world.*

It's not hard to see from the example above how epigenetics is impacting our children every day, and leaders in scientific research have taken notice. In 2008 the National Institutes of Health pledged $190 million to accelerate epigenetic research on illnesses including autism, bipolar disorder, schizophrenia, and asthma.

Dr. Michael Meaney: The Rock-Star of Genetics
The pioneer in this field of epigenetics is Dr. Michael Meaney, a

professor of neuroscience and psychiatry at McGill University in Montreal whose many awards include "Most Highly Cited Scientist" in neuroscience. Dr. Meaney's pioneering research on epigenetics has made him something of a rock star in the world of science, and the Dalai Lama himself follows Dr. Meaney's work, having met with him on several occasions. The Dalai Lama is interested in Dr. Meaney's research for the same reason today's parents should be interested. Dr. Meaney seems to have found a way to change our children's lives for the better. I am going to give you the Big Picture of his core research, and then discuss the implications for child health.

We all know that good parenting creates healthier kids, even if we don't exactly know how. But in his research with rats, Dr. Meaney may have discovered how.

The structure of the rat brain is very similar to the human brain. As Harvard's National Scientific Council wrote:

> Scientific knowledge in this area comes from research on animals as well as humans. These extensive bodies of work have generated common principles of developmental biology that support valid generalizations across species and reasonable hypotheses about humans based on consistent findings from animal studies. (Paper #3 Pg 2)

That's why Michael Meaney's research with rats has inspired so many neuroscientists: there is every reason to believe his findings apply to people, too.

Dr. Meaney's breakthrough began with the seemingly innocuous observation that calm, mellow rat mothers lick and groom their offspring much more frequently than rat mothers under stress, as first reported by scientists at Berkeley School of Public Health. Rat moms who frequently lick and groom their offspring tend to produce pups that learn better, explore their environment more freely, and show less fear. Most surprisingly, these calm rat pups continue to show this well-adjusted, healthy behavior throughout their entire lifetimes. It was as if the mother's licking "flipped a switch" in the rat pups' brains that rendered them calm for life.

But here's the big shocker: even when pups were cross-fostered (i.e., the calm moms were given a stressed mother's pups to raise), the effect on those foster-pups was the same: they were calmer, less fearful, less neurotic, and learned better, despite their neurotic genetic endowment. Not only did the calm mother's licking switch their own rat pups into calm mode for life, but it could do that in *any* rat pups, even the offspring of stressed mothers. And as an added bonus, these calm pups grew up to become calm mothers who in turn licked their offspring into calm status, and so on for many generations— happily ever after. And isn't that what we all want for our children?

"Desiree," a mother of three who lives in Washington state, was delighted when I explained to her the implications of Dr. Meaney's research:

> *YIPPEE! This is good news for me. I was unbelievably stressed while pregnant with my twins because I was continually warned that they would be very premature and I was in the hospital with all sorts of interventions to keep me pregnant. I can't do anything about that stress back then, but I can work on being the calmest mom possible right now.*

Why You Should Lick Your Children: Epigenetics After Birth

So, what does Dr. Meaney's research mean for parents? How does the rat's behavior translate to human beings? Meaney's research suggests that, regardless of our children's genes or their mental and physical problems, calm, attentive, and loving parenting can improve their children's health. Expressed in terms of the old Nature vs. Nurture debate, Nurture has *much* more impact on Nature than we thought, and can actually *trump* Nature in some cases. Kelly Mills of the Berkeley School of Public Health writes:

> *Rats raised by anxious mothers were far more likely to be fearful and prone to stress, despite their genetic makeup. And interestingly, this tendency towards anxiety stayed with the rats in adulthood. In contrast, the rats who were reared by calm mothers were themselves calmer and more inclined to explore new environments. This study demonstrated that*

*while genes are significant, early environment has a profound impact on
the expression or non-expression of those genes.*

But here's the twist: people tend to assume it's the mother's licking
that calms the rat pup. In fact, it is the calm mother's *calmness* that works
the miracle. Most people would assume the physical act of licking is what
causes the release of pleasant hormones in the baby rats' bloodstream. But
Dr. Meaney does not claim licking causes calmness. He describes licking
only as an "environmental signal." This means that licking is simply one way
the mother communicates that she is calm, because only calm mothers lick.
Mothers under stress don't lick, because they are in fight-or-flight mode, alert
to danger and busily sniffing and looking around for threats.

This distinction about environmental signals is important, because
we would be mistaken to assume that it is the physical contact of the mother
rat's tongue on the pup's fur that releases pleasant hormones. Rather, the
mother's lick is merely one of many environmental signals that reveal she is
calm. The pup's brain perceives these environmental signals as good news,
which triggers the release of beneficial hormones. To use a metaphor, it's
like Pavlov's Response. The dog doesn't have to see food to begin salivating.
He only has to hear the bell, an environmental signal that food is coming, to
begin salivating.

It's when we apply Meaney's research to parenting that we see how
important this distinction is. Parents might be tempted to believe that we can
get the same benefits in our children by doing the equivalent of licking our
children. For example, we might think that constant praise, or saying, "I love
you" to a child is the equivalent of a rat mother licking her pup. But we have
all witnessed anxious, overwrought parents who frequently praise their children
or say "I love you," yet neither the child nor the parent seems at all calm.

Another example: today's parents believe attending their child's
activities is a way to show love and build self-esteem, even though many
parents of a generation ago never attended their children's sporting events.
Yet somehow, their kids grew up knowing they were loved.

No, it's not so much how many sporting events we attend, or

how much attention we give our kids, or how many times we say, "I love you." It's not what we do or say. It's the environmental signals we give off without realizing it. It's the million things in our body-language and tone of voice that our kids are subconsciously monitoring. Kids don't monitor the behaviors we can control, like what we say or do; they monitor the environmental signals we cannot control. They are monitoring our level of stress and anxiety, because on a primal level, they instinctively intuit that their parent's stress levels are the true indication of how safe and secure they are.

The key word is "calm." Kids pick up on everything, and parents cannot fake being calm. Even if parents deceive themselves that they are calm, kids can always sense the stress level of a parent, because the emotional pipeline known as attunement never lies (as discussed in Chapter 3). So, kids know whether their parents are calm by the non-verbal communication they pick up—just like rat pups know their mother is calm because she licks them.

In a way, today's parents may have been kidding themselves that saying "I love you" or paying more attention to their children is the key to good parenting. We assume that kids want more attention and verbal reassurance of their parents' love. But if we actually asked our kids what they want, they would say something very different. At least, that is what Ellen Galinsky discovered. She is the president and co-founder of the Families and Work Institute, where she conducts research on the changing family, workplace, and community. Most children don't want to spend as much time with their parents as parents assume, she finds; they just want their parents *to be more relaxed* when they're together.

How Our Parenting Can Improve our Kids' Well-Being

Dr. Meaney's rat study should give us all hope, because it suggests that calm parenting can improve the health of our children, regardless of any genetic predisposition. That's because he found that the mechanism by which calm, mellow parenting produces well-adjusted, curious, eager-to-learn offspring is by affecting the rat pups' epigenomes.

When Dr. Meaney examined the brains of these calm rat pups, he discovered that their mother's licking had switched-on certain genes that helped control the stress-response in their little pup brains. As Dr. Meaney and his colleagues reported in a pioneering 2004 study, the rat pups were thus better able to regulate their stress response and stay calmer—for life. Science now knows how a parent's positive, calm nurture can set her offspring's development on a positive course for a lifetime.

In another article, Dr. Meaney describes studies of mother-offspring interactions in rats that demonstrate it is evolutionarily adaptive for an offspring to read a parent's reaction to their environment and switch-on or off the appropriate genes. Evolution has made rat pups very sensitive to their parents' stress levels, because reading the parents' tension gives them information crucial to their safety.

For example, if a parent is tense, the pup interprets this to mean that they are constantly on alert because their environment is very dangerous. In other words, the pup's developing brain assumes that if a parent has high levels of stress, it is because the parent's stress response is often being triggered. If the parent's stress response is being triggered, it must mean the place they live is dangerous, with many predators or enemies which they must fight or flee.

Accordingly, the rat pup's nervous system instinctively switches on genes that will render the pup quicker to react, and quicker to fight-or-flee. Thus, a rat mother under stress creates a rat pup with an over-sensitive stress-response, quick to overreact to threats—real or imagined.

Mother Nature did us a favor by making offspring sensitive to non-verbal cues of a parent's level of stress, because this sensitivity increases our chance of survival. That's why, from an evolutionary point of view, it makes perfect sense that kids notice everything.

What makes this news so important is that a child's epigenetics are influenced by the parent's environment, especially the level of stress in the parent's life. Stress and anxiety are believed to be a major influence on the switching-on or off of genes that cause illness, both mental and physical. Dr. Meaney's work thus suggests that if we reduce our stress, it will switch some of our children's "bad" genes off, and some of their "good" genes on.

This insight should leave parents asking the question, "How can

I be a good 'licker' of my children?" The short answer is that we need to reduce our stress, but the twist is that the best way to reduce our stress is not by reducing our activities. It is by socializing more with our spouses, relatives and friends. This will reduce the anxiety we don't even realize we have acquired in the past few decades of modern life. In Part 3, I will discuss this important point in detail, but next let's get clear on how epigenetics works.

How We Can Improve a Child's Health While Still in the Womb

Research suggests that stress during child development has a "sculpting" effect on our genes (both within the womb and in early childhood). In a normally developing child, some genes are switched-on and influence development of tissues, while others are switched off—having no impact on development. Many of the factors that can flip the switch are environmental, including stress. That is why Dr. Grafodatskaya (whose research on twins was discussed in Chapter 2) concludes that, in autism spectrum disorders, "both genetic and environmental factors likely play causative roles, influencing fetal or early postnatal brain development, directly or via epigenetic modifications."

For example, Duke Department of Medicine researcher Simon Gregory has found that a particular "social" gene is often switched off in ASD (autism spectrum disorder) children, as he described in a paper published in October 2009 in the journal *BMC Medicine*.

Most genetic studies of autism focus on variations in the DNA sequence itself, especially on genes that are missing. Gregory and his colleagues looked at an oxytocin receptor gene, called OXTR, and found that about 70 percent of the 119 autistic people in his study had a methylated (i.e., "switched-off") OXTR gene. In a control group of people without autism, the rate was about 40 percent. Oxytocin is a hormone that affects social interaction; difficulty relating to others is common for those with autism spectrum disorders.

Of course, more research is necessary. But Gregory says methylation-modifying drugs might be a new avenue for the treatment of autism. He also hopes that his findings will provide a new tool for doctors to diagnose autism.

"Methylation has been very hot in the cancer field for a number of years," Gregory says. "To find something like this associated with autism is very exciting."

Dr. Gregory's research helps to explain why there is no single "asthma gene" or "autism gene." More likely, a child may carry multiple genes that contribute to autism, for example, and epigenetic switches turn those genes on (or off), which may lead to symptoms of autism.

You may recall that in Chapter 2 we examined Dr. Beversdorf's research on the timing of prenatal stress on programming a fetus. His research team also has studied the genes involved in neurodevelopmental disorders. One study in particular offers parents insight into how stress programs children's social behavior through epigenetics and switching genes on or off.

Dr. Beversdorf's team figured there must be a certain gene (or genes) that plays an important role in controlling reaction to stress in both humans and mice. Other research had shown that when the gene *5-HTT* stops working properly in the part of our brains responsible for our stress-response, then humans tend to lose some self-control and overreact to stress.

Dr. Beversdorf's team was able to create a kind of "artificial epigenetic effect" in certain mice, essentially switching off this calming gene and creating easily-stressed female mice. This allowed them to study whether switching-off one of the calming genes of a mother rat might create a high incidence of autistic behaviors in her offspring.

It is very difficult to actually methylate, or switch off, a specific gene, so the researchers found a way to mimic this process. Through careful breeding, they produced female mice lacking the 5-HTT gene. This process imitates epigenetics, in that these female rats now acted as if their 5-HTT gene had been switched-off.

These easily-stressed, "switched-off 5-HTT" females were then impregnated and put in moderately stressful conditions. Researchers kept another group of pregnant mommy mice that had the 5-HTT gene switched-on. These mice, serving as a control group, were exposed to neutral, non-stressful conditions so they could be compared to the switched-off 5-HTT mice mothers later.

The "switched-off 5-HTT" mother mice's offspring showed significantly more anti-social and autism-like behaviors than the control group of offspring whose mothers had been exposed to neutral conditions. Beversdorf's team concluded that prenatal stress combined with epigenetics (in this case, a calming gene was "switched-off") appeared to create symptoms of autism in the offspring of these mice.

This supports Dr. Meaney's theory about epigenetic changes to genes in developing offspring: it shows that stress in the rat mother appears to program the rat fetus. The fetus absorbs the increased stress hormones in the womb, which switches off a gene that keeps rats calm.

Thus the rat fetus is programmed to be constantly on the alert, with an overreactive stress response. If this baby rat is born into an environment that is truly dangerous, then switching off this calming gene may be a valuable adaptation. But if the mother has an overreactive stress-response, then her offspring develop the same problem.

Dr. Beversdorf's study is a good example of the impact that stressed parents unknowingly have on their children. Even if we are not aware of our sensitivity to stressors, our over-reactions to situations may create enough stress to program our children's stress-response as well, and this can continue on down the line for generations. It may never have occurred to us just how much our stress affects our children's development, but from an evolutionary point of view, Dr. Beversdorf's experiment results make perfect sense, as Dr. James Potash of Johns Hopkins University argues.

From his research on mice, Dr. Potash suspects that prenatal stress has impacted our ancestors for thousands of years, and serves an evolutionary purpose. In particular, stress hormones leave their mark on the epigenome of DNA that is active in the brain. Dr. Potash believes that the influence of stress on the epigenome evolved as a survival of the fittest feature, because it helped animals to be better prepared for future threats. "If you think of the stress system as preparing you for fight-or-flight, you might imagine that these epigenetic changes might prepare you to fight harder or flee faster the next time you encounter something stressful," says Dr. Potash. We will discuss this evolutionary aspect in Chapter 7.

These behaviors may have outlived their usefulness, however. Whereas our ancestors could flee that saber-toothed tiger, there are many modern stressors that we cannot flee so readily, such as work deadlines or a stressful marriage. This means that today's pregnant women may end up more chronically stressed than Mother Nature intended, and they pass this stress onto their babies. These stress hormones are one of the triggers of the epigenome on a child's genes, so stress directly impacts a child's genetic predisposition to a whole spectrum of ailments (much more on this in Chapter 5).

Happy Ending: Epigenetics Are At Least Partially Reversible

As discussed above, the research of Dr. Meaney and others suggests that, if parents reduce their stress levels, not only does this prevent further damage to their children's genes, but some genes can actually reverse their "switching" and heal. New studies show that as identical twins age, for instance, their epigenomes become less and less alike. As a result, one identical twin may develop schizophrenia while the other does not; one may develop a strongly genetic form of breast cancer while the other does not. The reason is that some fortunate event in the healthy twin's life may have turned off genes associated with disease.

That suggests that harmful epigenetics can not only be prevented, but can perhaps even be reversed. Children are not doomed by the DNA their parents passed on to them. It appears we can undo, at least in part, the effects of epigenetics on mental or physical illness through things like diet, exercise, socializing more, and training our minds to create less stress and anxiety in our lives.

As Dr. Curt Sandman argues, there are grounds for considerable optimism:

> One possibility is that a high-quality postnatal environment will reverse the negative effects of prenatal stress. There is compelling evidence from animal models that the negative effects of prenatal maternal stress can be attenuated [i.e., reduced] by high-quality postnatal maternal care. Consistent with these studies, there are a few recent studies with humans that suggest that the provision of high quality maternal care may

ameliorate the negative effects of prenatal stress on fearful temperament,
stress regulation and cognitive functioning.

He believes that, like the "good licking rat moms" in Dr. Meaney's research, humans get a second chance. Even if pre-natal stress caused some epigenetic damage in the womb, calm and positive parenting can heal that damage.

But what does Dr. Sandman mean by "high-quality maternal care"? It is not necessarily how much time we spend with our child, or how frequently we say, "I love you." It's more about our level of calm, casual behavior—something we cannot fake. The lower our stress response, the fewer verbal cues parents pass on to their children, so kids' stress response stays lower, too.

Again: it's not so much what we say or do to our kids; it's more about the "vibe" we give off in their presence. We simply cannot fake being calm to our kids, so we need to reduce our stress levels. As I will explain in later chapters, the more we socialize, with spouse, family and friends, the calmer we will be around our kids.

Both human and animal studies suggest that, even if offspring are born with a tendency toward overreaction and fear that might suppress their ability to learn and socialize, calmer parenting will "switch on" enough of the "good" genes to repair some of the damage. "'I've got goose bumps right now talking about it,' says Randy Jirtle to the Los Angeles Times. Dr. Jirtle studies epigenetics at Duke University Medical Center in Durham, N.C. 'You're looking at the book of life, how it's read and how you can change it.'"

This epigenetic research holds such promise that the National Institutes of Health recently launched the National Children's Study, which will follow over 100,000 families all across America. It will collect data to chart how prenatal exposure to toxins and stress is linked to a child's health all the way into adulthood.

Money talks, and the government's commitment of millions of dollars shows just how promising it is in reducing or preventing many disorders and illnesses in children. Experts estimate that, for example, every child with autism will cost the parents about $2 million over a lifetime, plus roughly 1,000 hours per year of extra care, not to mention the roughly $50,000 per year the community will pay in support services—and Harvard research also points out the detrimental effect on our future workforce.

But most importantly, this stress research means that hundreds of thousands of families may be able to avoid or at least lessen the mental and physical illnesses their children face. Imagine the powerful impact that can have on all of us. Whereas we cannot prevent things like the death of a loved one or genetic predisposition, we can identify those pregnancies (and/or households) at higher risk for epigenetic problems and target them for special care.

This kind of preventive medicine would be a compassionate and relatively inexpensive way to optimize prenatal care and reduce maternal stress, thereby reducing the number of future disease diagnoses. In the words of "Gail," a mother of an autistic boy named "James":

> *I worry that when I die, the burden of taking care of James will lie solely on the shoulders of my daughter, Annie. And more than that, I worry that he'll be put in an institution and die alone. And I worry that we can barely afford to keep our house on our present income—how are we going to save enough so he has a trust to live on after we're gone?*

A tiny investment in prenatal care could save huge amounts in life-long special services. Children's health is in crisis today. We need to pull our heads out of the sand and realize how stress is affecting our children in ways that evolution never intended.

To sum up this chapter, scientists have identified the mechanisms by which stress can harm our children's health. During a child's development, both in the womb and postnatally, stress affects the epigenome, switching some "good" genes off and some "bad" genes on. The key insight of this chapter is how a parent's stress can get "under the skin" of a child. Stress can interact with the epigenome, changing the behavior of genes and contributing to the creation of a disorder.

But that's not the end of the story.

It is crucial for every parent to understand that stress affects *every* child—it's simply a matter of degree. As we'll see in the next chapter, epigenetics appears to play a role in many of the child disorders that have become epidemic today. From colic and food allergies to obesity and asthma, stress seems to be a risk factor in child disorders in a dose-response manner. The more stressed-out a household is, the greater a child's symptoms.

Fortunately, epigenetic status is at least partially reversible, and the more we understand, the better we can shape our children's health. In Chapter 5, we will learn just how widespread the epigenetic effect of stress actually is.

Chapter 5

Parental Stress Affects Almost Every Child—It's Just a Matter of Degree

In the U.S., and Britain, the rate of obesity in children has risen more than 40 percent over the last 15 years to become an epidemic. In these two countries, more than half of adults are overweight or obese. What is at the root of this phenomenon? Genetics alone cannot possibly account for it, since genes do not change nearly fast enough for, say, a fat-gene mutation to sweep through the population.

It appears that prenatal stress affects a child's genes that influence obesity. It's as if the fetus is saying to itself, "Wow! There seem to be a lot of stress hormones crossing Mom's placenta into my womb, here. She must live in a stressful environment; perhaps she's stressed because the hunting and gathering aren't going so well this season, and our tribe faces starvation. I'd better adapt my body to store the most fat I can from every tidbit of food that comes my way after I'm born."

Therefore, the fetus uses epigenetics to switch certain genes on, and certain other genes off, programming its metabolism to absorb and preserve every calorie it can in what it assumes will be an environment of scarcity and adversity upon birth.

In one study of more than 65,000 children, for instance, Dr. Jiong Li of Denmark's University of Aarhus found that mothers who were stressed because they lost a close relative just before their pregnancy were two to three times more likely to give birth to a child who would be obese by age 13.

Why would a pregnant woman's stress make her child obese? Apparently, the fetus mistakenly assumes that a mother's high level of stress hormones passing through the placenta means food is scarce, so the fetus adapts by slowing down its metabolism, storing more fat, and seeking more food.

The unfortunate result is that obesity-prone babies are born to American parents who have plenty of food. In America we don't want our children storing more fat or seeking more food, but the fetus can be duped by the sheer number of stress hormones in the womb.

But how could the human fetus have evolved to make such a serious error in adaptation? Why would Mother Nature allow the next generation of kids to develop disorders because of their parents' stress?

In fact, Mother Nature had the best of intentions when she gave us an evolutionary tool to help the fetus prepare for the world it would soon be born into. If the fetus could anticipate the kinds of challenges it would face in its upcoming environment, it could hit the ground running when it was born. Mother Nature's evolutionary tool is called the "predictive adaptive response,"

The predicative adaptive response can be divided into 3 parts:

1) *Predictive*: In order to make its predictions about the outside world, the fetus picks up on hormonal "cues" from its mother, such as how many stress hormones are crossing her placenta. For example, if there are a high number of stress hormones, the fetus interprets that to mean that Mom is often afraid because the outside environment must be particularly hostile.

2) *Adaptive*: The fetal brain starts throwing the switches and pulling the levers of the epigenomes to adapt fetal development, and steer it towards a custom-tailored brain and body.

3) *Response*: This custom-tailored baby will hopefully respond better to the challenges it predicted it would face after it is born.

The problem is, the predictive adaptive response has not turned out to be as "adaptive" to our modern society as Mother Nature had hoped, because it offers only clumsy, blunt solutions to the challenges of our modern lifestyle. These solutions end up being worse than the original problem. Imagine if you found a mouse in your home, screeched in horror, and then purchased 150 cats to make sure you never saw a mouse again. No more mice, but now you have a cat problem. This lack of nuance is what the predictive adaptive response looks like when it tries to "solve" the problem of too many stress hormones in the womb.

Here is the key point of this chapter: It is absolutely crucial that we understand the predictive adaptive response (and its unintended consequences) because the predictive adaptive response is what links parental stress to most child disorders, from colic to autism—it's just a matter of degree.

You may remember Dr. Dennis Kinney, director of the Genetics Laboratory at Harvard Medical School, from Chapter 2. His point is so important that it bears repeating: "prenatal stress does not need to be either chronic or extremely severe in order to have a significant effect on postnatal development. While stronger effects on behavior will usually result from more severe and prolonged prenatal exposure to stress, significant and lasting effects have been produced by rather moderate and brief exposures to stress."

In this chapter, we will discuss the evidence linking parental stress to minor child disorders like colic. We will also examine medical studies linking parental stress to more severe child disorders like diabetes, asthma and ASD (autism spectrum disorder). The common denominator in this wide spectrum of child disorders is parental stress, and the evidence suggests that, generally speaking, the more stress hormones in the womb, the greater the risk of a serious child disorder. I'm not saying that parental stress is the only cause of this wide array of disorders, but I am saying that parental stress is a significant risk factor in a dose-response manner, i.e., the more stress a child absorbs in the womb, the greater the risk of an ailment, and the greater the probable severity of the ailment.

Of course, it is easiest to spot how the predictive adaptive response has gone awry in the most extreme cases, where a serious mental or physical problem emerges. For example, parental stress has been linked to asthma, children's diabetes, depression and neurodevelopmental disorders. But every parent needs to be aware that their stress may be affecting their children's health even in milder ways, such as colic, learning disabilities, and allergies. Therefore, let's look at how this process works.

The Predictive Adaptive Response

Stress is a normal, essential part of life, so we should hardly be surprised that most animals, including humans, evolved to have a stress response. Stress protects us by causing us to worry and anticipate potential dangers, and to trigger our fight-or-flight response to address those threats. Stress motivates us to meet deadlines and achieve goals, to prepare for the upcoming harsh winter, and to do what needs to be done to care for our loved ones.

It makes sense that evolution would give babies a stress response that could help them adjust to their environment. Dr. Meaney's licking rat mothers, you will recall from Chapter 4, were calm because there were no threats around and therefore they licked their offspring. Then, the baby rats take this licking as a cue to switch their stress-responses into low gear. But if the mothers were stressed and in fight-or-flight mode, they would not lick their offspring, so the pups' stress-response would presumably kick into high gear.

Likewise with humans. If there are few stress hormones *in utero*, the stress response of the fetus remains in low gear. But if the fetus is surrounded by many stress hormones, he or she will be born extra-alert, with an extra-sensitive stress system, to increase the odds of survival. Consider an experiment conducted right after an earthquake, where 28 panic-stricken pregnant women, between 18 and 36 weeks gestation, were monitored by ultrasound. The experiment found

> that all fetuses showed intense hyperkinesia [i.e., much movement]
> lasting between 2 and 8 hours, with numerous, disordered and vigorous

movements. These studies provide compelling evidence that maternal
stress has direct and immediate effects on fetal physiology and behavior.

This is a dramatic example of the sensitivity of the fetus to hormonal cues following a genuine crisis. Unfortunately, however, our children's predictive adaptive response has only one, clumsy reaction when it senses high stress levels: overreact, as if the sky is falling.

For example, let's return to the illustration at the beginning of this chapter, where a fetus is "talking to itself." We would like for that fetus to have options, saying something like: "Hmm. There seem to be a lot of stress hormones crossing Mom's placenta into my bloodstream. I can see at least two possible scenarios: Mom may be stressed because she's short of food. Or, perhaps she's stressed simply because being stressed-out is the New Normal in this day and age. I'll boot up my trusty predictive adaptive response to find out which scenario applies, then adapt my development accordingly, in a lovely, nuanced manner."

That's what we *wish* babies were thinking to themselves in the womb. Unfortunately, the predictive adaptive response is more of a blunt object than a sophisticated laptop. Civilized society has developed much faster than our stress-response machinery has evolved, leaving us in an unprecedented situation where we have sky-high stress levels but low danger levels in our actual, day-to-day living.

In our caveman days, the fetus could safely predict that many stress hormones *in utero* probably meant the fetus would be born into scarcity. This blunt reaction did not require any nuance back when humans lived as hunter-gatherers. Perhaps the predictive adaptive response allowed new-born babies to "hit the ground running," and this helped our species survive and thrive. But today, this adaptation has outlived its usefulness, and our children are paying the price because evolution has mistakenly programmed them to be overreactive. It's like, "Predictive Adaptive Response Gone Wild."

For example, in 2002, a review of more than 200 research papers concluded that the stress of overreactive parents tends to "…create vulnerabilities and/or interact with genetically based vulnerabilities [i.e., epigenetics] in offspring that…lead to consequent accumulating risk for mental health disorders, major chronic diseases, and early mortality." In other words, parental stress hormones in the womb trigger the predictive adaptive response to mobilize a "defense" that ends up being worse than the perceived threat. What the predictive adaptive response creates as a solution may end up becoming a child disorder, and the more stress a child absorbs, the greater the likelihood of disorders—from minor to severe.

The predictive adaptive response is so crucial to raising healthy children that parents need to understand how it works. Knowledge is power, and parents can reduce their stress levels during pregnancy if they understand how their stress affects the health of their child *in utero*. And remember that it's never too late to begin to reverse the effects with calmer parenting.

In the next section, we will follow the process by which stress in a parent's mind somehow "gets under a child's skin" to become a disorder. We will trace the stress hormones in a mother's bloodstream as they journey across the placenta and alter the epigenomes of the fetal brain, such that a disorder is created and continues to grow after the baby is born.

To better learn this process, we will use an oversimplified metaphor of the womb as a construction site where babies are built. We will picture the predictive adaptive response as the foreman of this baby construction site, and sometimes the foreman make mistakes and builds structures the architect never intended.

The Womb is a Construction Site, with the Predictive Adaptive Response as "Foreman"

Like many other processes in our bodies, the stress response relies on dozens of genes to do its work. Think of each gene as a worker on a construction site, building a stress response for a baby who will be born soon. These gene workers must fulfill their specific role and cooperate well to make sure the stress response works properly: for example, some genes work in the crew in charge of Worrying About Danger, trying to anticipate potential threats. Some genes work in the Fight-or-Flight Crew, triggering this response when appropriate. Yet other genes work in the Regulatory Crew, with the very important job of calming down their baby's stress response when there's no longer a need to flip out.

The predictive adaptive response (I'll just call it "PAR" from now on) is like the construction foreman of all these work crews. But the PAR doesn't manage its crews with thoughtful, nuanced language; PAR manages by barking orders at these gene-workers: "You! Start working now! ...Hey! You over there! Stop working now!" The PAR can only shape the construction of the fetal stress-response by epigenetics—switching on the helpful worker-genes, and switching off the destructive worker genes. You might say PAR is hot-tempered and impulsive.

That's why the PAR offers only a clumsy response to nuanced situations. For example, if a pregnant woman is stressed, and many stress hormones cross her placenta into the baby's "construction site," the PAR foreman only has two possible sets of building plans. So, given the high number of stress hormones, he figures this baby will be born into a harsh environment, so he throws away the plans for a calm stress response and builds a very sensitive, overreactive stress-response. To do so, perhaps he barks orders that some of the genes in the Regulatory Crew should switch off and stop calming things down so much. Then he barks orders that more genes in the Fight-or-Flight Crew should switch on and start working overtime. But, to make sure his fetus can "hit the ground running" upon birth, the PAR orders the greatest number of gene-workers to switch-on and start working on the Worrying About Danger Crew.

This is what I mean when I talk about how stress epigenetically switches some "bad" genes on, and some "good" genes off, as discussed in Chapter 4. In this illustration, the "good" genes are the Regulatory Crew, who usually would help a baby to calm down when appropriate, postnatally. With too few Regulatory Genes on the job, the newborn child will remain chronically stressed. In addition, since there are so many Worrying About Danger genes switched on and working overtime, they become "bad" genes because they have the baby constantly overreacting to stimuli as if all stimuli were potential threats.

This overreactive baby will have a more difficult time navigating life because his stress-response system was programmed *in utero* for a stressful scenario that doesn't exist. The PAR foreman thought all those stress hormones meant the baby would face tremendous danger. In fact, the baby will just be born into a highly-stressed lifestyle, the New Normal of today. So, the baby is now stuck with the worst adaptation possible—an overreactive stress-response in a highly-stressed environment (of course, this is an over-simplified example for the purpose of illustration).

The PAR Only Offers Clumsy Solutions that are Worse than the Original Problem

Here is the key point: The PAR doesn't do a nuanced analysis of the environment the mother is living in, so as to make an accurate prediction of the tools the baby will need to survive outside the womb. The PAR doesn't send out scouts, consult focus groups, or poll the mother's friends and neighbors to see what kind of stress-response would best suit the fetus's upcoming environment. The PAR simply bases its design on how many stress hormones surround the fetal construction site in the womb, then starts barking orders to the epigenomes.

The only variance the PAR can offer is the question of degree of reactivity of the stress-response. Again, to oversimplify, if ten stress hormones cross the placenta onto the PAR's building site, the PAR will only switch on five Worrying About Danger gene-workers, and only switch-off five Calming Down gene-workers. And perhaps that baby will develop ADHD as it gets older. Or if, say, 50 stress hormones cross the placenta to show up on the construction site, then the PAR will switch-on 25 Worrying About Danger genes, and switch-off 25 Calming Down gene workers; so perhaps that baby might go on to develop allergies or diabetes. But if 100 maternal stress hormones appear at the construction site, the PAR foreman builds his most sensitive, overreactive stress-response, with maximum Worry About Danger genes, and very few Calm Down genes, and this child may develop asthma or autism.

In other words, a fetus will be equipped by the PAR with either a standard stress response, using standard levels of alertness and standard levels of calming, or with an oversensitive stress response, which chronically overreacts to perceived threats, and calms itself down only rarely and with great difficulty. The question of *how* overreactive the child's stress response will be is merely a matter of degree, based on how many maternal stress hormones were encountered in the womb.

Let's repeat the above sentence, because its implications are significant: The more stress hormones there are *in utero*, the more overreactive the fetal stress-response and immune response will be, and therefore the more severe the subsequent disorder will be (NB: the *immune response* is the body's ability to fight off bacteria, viruses, allergens, and such).

This is the dose-response concept we have discussed earlier, in Chapters 1 and 2. To give an example in the simplest of terms, a "few" maternal stress hormones in the womb may trigger the PAR to increase the sensitivity of the baby's stress response, leading to colic. With the addition of "a few more" maternal stress hormones, the fetus may then be vulnerable to tantrums and acting-out behavior, but grows out of this in the first year or two of life. However, if the PAR of another fetus encounters yet a few more stress hormones in its womb, it may produce a slightly more reactive stress response, such that the newborn baby goes on to develop learning delays, because the anxious chatter in its brain precludes easy learning.

In other words, for every fetus with a PAR that encounters one degree more of maternal stress hormones, the predictive adaptive response may produce a stress response that is one degree more overreactive, which predisposes the baby to a disorder one degree more serious.

Of course, the process is not as black-and-white as I have depicted it. And other risk factors are involved—stress is not the only one. But the effect of stress on the epigenetic process of a child's developing brain has been proven by many studies.

Some of the Evidence Linking PAR and Neurodevelopmental Disorders

UC Irvine's Dr. Curt Sandman and colleagues recently demonstrated how prenatal stress triggers the predictive adaptive response, which affects the development of the fetal brain in ways that were still apparent when the children were between 6 and 9 years of age.

Researchers measured the anxiety levels experienced by 35 women who were pregnant in 2002. When these women's offspring reached at least 6 years of age, the children's brain development was analyzed by an MRI scan. The children of mothers who showed high anxiety at 19 weeks of gestation tended to have less developed brains at age 6. Specifically, the regions of the brain responsible for regulating their stress-response reactivity and their learning capacity were smaller.

In 2007 Dr. Sandman and Elysia Poggi-Davis conducted a study at the University of California-Davis. They measured 247 mothers' levels of anxiety and salivary cortisol (an indicator of stress) three times during their pregnancy and once after they gave birth. Then, when these mothers' newborns were two months old, the doctors measured the mothers' fear reactivity levels.

The scientists found that elevated maternal cortisol at 30-to-32 weeks of gestation was strongly associated with more negative reactivity in the infant, which suggests that prenatal stress affects the development of infant temperament.

Dr. Sandman concludes: "The accumulating evidence supports the conclusion that fetal exposure to stress profoundly influences the nervous system, with consequences that persist into childhood and perhaps beyond."

In another example, England's University of Bristol launched a long-term project to gather data on over 7,000 babies born in the County of Avon between 1991-1992 and their parents. The researchers had no specific research agenda. Like the government workers in Dr. Kinney's Louisiana Storms study from Chapter 2, these researchers had nothing to prove and no specific agenda—in scientific parlance, they had no "confirmatory bias." Instead, they were simply trying to assemble a thorough database on these children, which could then be analyzed by scientists around the world to answer their various research questions.

And analyze they did. In 2002, Drs. Vivette Glover (Professor of Perinatal Psychobiology at Imperial College London) and Tom O'Connor (Professor of Psychiatry at the University of Rochester Medical School) used this database to assess the effect of maternal anxiety on the long-term behavior of children. Of the 7,448 children whose files they analyzed, both boys and girls were roughly twice as likely to display symptoms of ADHD if their mothers had felt anxiety during their pregnancy. They found "strong and significant links" between a woman's anxiety level during pregnancy and behavioral problems of her child at age four. They concluded that the prenatal stress hormones in the womb appear to have a direct effect on fetal brain development.

In a similar undertaking, the Kennedy Krieger Institute at Johns Hopkins Medical School created the Interactive Autism Network, a website database where families with an autistic child could register and provide researchers with their family data. In the first year, over 10,000 families registered.

One of the patterns that emerged from studying these 10,000 families was a very high rate of maternal depression—over half of these 10,000 mothers of autistic children experienced depression. Researchers had long known about the high prevalence of anxiety and depression among these moms, but they made the same assumptions the public continues to make: parental depression was caused by the tremendous emotional challenges of caring for an autistic child.

But Kennedy Krieger's database showed that, in fact, over half these mothers were diagnosed with anxiety and depression even before their autistic child was born. Julie Daniels of UNC Chapel Hill published the same conclusion in the prestigious "Pediatrics" research journal. Daniels compared 1,227 families with autistic children to more than 30,000 non-autistic families and found that depression and mental disorders were much higher in mothers of autistic children, and these disorders were diagnosed even before the autistic child was born.

It is becoming clear that depressed mothers, through no fault of their own, involuntarily pass their anxiety onto their babies, beginning in the womb, as the National Scientific Council for the Developing Child explains:

> *Indeed, there is increasing evidence that effects on stress-response systems*
> *are one mechanism linking maternal depression to the child's own risk*
> *of developing depression and other emotional disorders. When mothers*
> *are depressed, both early in a child's life and later, their children tend to*

produce higher and more fluctuating levels of stress chemicals such as
cortisol. (Pg 4)

To paraphrase the above quote, maternal stress hormones affect the development of the baby's stress-response, both inside the womb and outside. Consequently, the baby may be born with an oversensitive, overreactive stress response that produces too many stress hormones. These stress hormones then trigger the child's fight-or-flight response too often, which in turn leads to the socially-impaired behavior characteristic of autism, ADHD, and other developmental disorders.

Harvard's National Scientific Council emphasizes just how serious the consequences will be if we don't provide treatment to stop this vicious circle. If we don't screen pregnant women for stress, the effects carry into future generations because overreactive parents create overreactive children:

Because chronic and severe maternal depression has potentially far-reaching harmful effects on families and children, its widespread occurrence can undermine the future prosperity and well-being of society as a whole. When children grow up in an environment of mental illness, the development of their brains may be seriously weakened, with implications for their ability to learn as well as for their own later physical and mental health. (Pg 1)

And more than one study has confirmed the National Scientific Council's assertion. The implications of this research are significant, because it affirms the assertion of Columbia's Dr. Catherine Monk, discussed in Chapter 2, that doctors should be screening mothers for depression and stress during pregnancy, the way pregnant women are screened for diabetes.

Let me be clear that the mother is not to blame for her child's disorders. In Part 2 of this book, I will discuss at length how a parent's relationships, her flight-response within those relationships, and the resulting isolation are largely responsible for parental stress, which in turn harms a child's stress response, but let me give you a brief preview:

Among the studies showing why a mother's depression is not simply her fault, was one by scientists at the University of Queensland. These scientists followed more than 3,500 Australian families for 21 years, from birth of a child through age 21. The results were startling. Whereas many people assume that a depressed spouse leads to marital breakdown, this study suggests it may be the other way around: marital quality may be a big factor in maternal depression, which in turn contributes to the long-term health outcome of the child. In other words, the mother is not to blame for her depression or her child's subsequent health problems.Later in this book, I will present more compelling evidence to show that a mother's stress is closely linked to her marriage and social support network. You may have heard the expression, "It takes a village to raise a child." I would say at the very least that it takes an extended family to raise a child, and parenting is much more of a tribal or team effort than we realize.

Now that we have examined how the predictive adaptive response contributes to child neurological disorders, let's take a closer look at another kind of child-disorder: immune-disorders.

How the Predictive Adaptive Response Causes Immune Disorders

We have now arrived at the second stage of our journey through the Land of the Predictive Adaptive Response. To sum up this chapter so far, I have discussed how sometimes, the PAR's solution turns out to be worse than the problem. The predictive adaptive response may interpret too many stress hormones in the womb as meaning there is great danger in the outside world, and it is this danger that causes the mother's spike in stress hormones. The predictive adaptive response jumps to the conclusion that the baby will have to be constantly on guard. Therefore the predictive adaptive response programs the baby's stress response to overreact to stimuli and behave impulsively. In our caveman days, perhaps this oversensitive stress response would have helped the child react quickly to perceived enemies or predators. But, in today's safer but more anxious world, this overreactive stress response, is characteristic of many social, cognitive, behavior, and neurodevelopmental disorders in children.

However, an overreactive stress response is only one of the clumsy solutions the PAR offers. There is also the overreactive immune response.

The predictive adaptive response can also interpret too many stress hormones in the womb to mean there are many plagues and toxins in the outside world, and it is fear of these toxins that caused the spike in the mother's stress hormones. The predictive adaptive response then jumps to the conclusion that the child needs a particularly sensitive immune system to help nip any infection in the bud, such as plagues, contagious diseases, or wounds from fighting. Therefore, the predictive adaptive response programs the baby's immune response to overreact to perceived toxins. But in today's medically-advanced world, an oversensitive, overreactive immune response finds toxins where there are none, leading to immune disorders, such as allergies, asthma and diabetes.

For example, Harvard's National Scientific Council uses the stress of maternal depression to describe how the fetus' predictive adaptive response can affect both the stress-response and the immune response of a child:

> *It is not commonly understood that even very young children are likely to be affected by their mother's depression and these effects may be lasting. Adverse effects may even begin during pregnancy. As noted earlier, maternal depression in the prenatal period is linked to alterations in the* **stress response and immune systems** *of the fetus…* *[Emphasis added] (Page 7)*

In other words, the predictive adaptive response affects not only the development of the stress response, but also the immune system. Next we'll take a look at some of the evidence.

In 2008, Drs. Michael Meaney (our "rock star" from Chapter 4 on epigenetics) and Moshe Szyf wrote that the increase of asthma and type-2 diabetes in our society has been too dramatic to dismiss as simply genetic. It appears they were right.

In Australia, Dr. John Henderson is finding the same alarming trend linking parental stress to child allergies and asthma. In his pediatric practice at Sir Charles Gairdner Hospital in Perth, he treats children with asthma, and it was his encounters with so many asthmatic kids that inspired his research, in hopes of finding and treating causes of asthma rather than just treating its symptoms.

Dr. Henderson noticed how often children would tell him that a stressful event triggered their asthma attacks, and he was intrigued to read research reports that prenatal stress could be a predictor of a child's asthma later in life. The research literature also reported a marked increase in asthma in richer nations, much more than in developing countries.

You might think that poverty and disease should mean higher stress levels in poor countries, but perhaps they have stronger social and family support networks than in developed countries, and social support may trump money in terms of reducing stress levels. In any event, Dr. Henderson's observation of his patient's families and his general impression were that we are much more isolated and anxious in developed countries than we used to be, and our children experience more asthma as a result. (In Chapter 6 we'll examine how isolation has increased our stress).

So, he decided to test his theory. Dr. Henderson, co-author Hannah Cookson, and their team set out to analyze the cases in a database of 5,810 children with asthma in Avon County, England, looking in particular at whether there was a relationship between the mothers' anxiety levels during their pregnancy and the chance that their child would have asthma at age 7. Even after the team factored out other influences, such as maternal smoking, the children of anxious mothers were 64 percent more likely to develop asthma, in a *dose-response* manner. Recall that dose-response means that the higher the mothers' anxiety measures, the more likely their children would develop asthma.

This dose-response finding is significant, because it supports the theory that parental stress affects every child: it's just a matter of degree. You may recall that Dr. Dennis Kinney's findings from the Louisiana storms in Chapter 2 also showed a dose-response relationship. This means the more severe the storm (i.e., the "dose"), the greater the number of children who developed ASD (i.e., the "response"). Likewise with Dr. Henderson's research: the greater the mother's anxiety, the more likely her child would develop asthma. More research needs to be done, but the implication is that, if we tested for other ailments in Dr. Kinney's Louisiana children or Dr. Henderson's Australia children, we would find higher rates of colic, learning disabilities, ADHD, or allergies, also in a dose-dependent manner.

Dr. Rosalind Wright of Harvard Medical School agrees with Dr. Henderson's research on asthma. She published a 2007 study and 2008 review of the medical literature on prenatal stress, which revealed a strong parallel in the results of research on both animals and humans. Dr. Wright shares the growing belief that maternal stress hormones cross the placenta and trigger the predictive adaptive response to influence the immune system of the fetus to become overreactive, producing the inflamed tissue and bronchial passages that characterize allergies or asthma once the child is born.

Let's sum up what we've seen so far in this chapter. The PAR is the well-meaning if bumbling leader of the prenatal stage in a child's life, assessing the parent's stress levels from the number of stress hormones in the womb, and adjusting development via epigenetic mechanisms that switch genes on or off. But the PAR continues to influence the development of a child's brain and immune system long after the baby is born.

For example, a study of more than 8,000 children found that both maternal and paternal anxiety were associated with a child developing recurrent abdominal pain. Scientists led by Dr. Paul Ramchandani, a senior research fellow in Child Psychiatry at Oxford University in England, collected data from 8,272 participants to see whether parental stress during a child's first year of life was a factor in later onset of recurrent stomach aches. They found that, for mothers who tested as anxious six months after the birth of their child, that child was 53 percent more likely to have chronic stomach aches at age six. For anxious fathers, the child was 38 percent more likely to have recurring abdominal pain at age six.

After the child is born, the process of PAR continues, but obviously, the PAR no longer gets its information from counting maternal stress hormones in the womb. Instead, it relies on the attunement we discussed in Chapter 3. Attunement is that emotional pipeline of non-verbal communication between parent and child, who can read each other's feelings, often "catching" emotions the way we catch a virus. And anxious parents may be sending plenty of stress through that emotional pipeline, as we will see in Chapter 6.

Chapter 6
Stress Outside the Womb

You may recall in Chapter 1 I mentioned the "Scale of Stress," an imaginary graph. If we could measure and chart a family's stress levels, each family might appear as a dot somewhere between 0 and 100 on the graph. Near the "Zero-Stress" end of the scale would be the dots of those rare families that are blissful. On the other end of the scale would be the more-stressed, more-isolated or chaotic families, who show up as dots near the "100% Stressed" end of the continuum.

Of course, most of our families fall somewhere between these two extremes, but the important point here is the degree of risk. The higher a family falls on such a Scale of Stress, the greater the odds that stress affects a child's health. Parental stress is a factor in almost every child's behavior; it is simply a matter of degree.

Note that this is an extreme oversimplification, but let's imagine for the sake of illustration that blissful parents who fall in the "0 to 20" portion of the scale of stress have children with mild symptoms, such as colic. Perhaps the parents on the "20 to 40" section have kids with severe tantrums, but they grow out of it. In the "40 to 60" range are children with ADHD or allergies. "60 to 80" has children with diabetes, and "80 to 100" has children with asthma or neurodevelopmental disorders.

Of course, this scale is an oversimplified illustration because these disorders do not fall in neat little black-and-white categories, and parental stress is only one risk factor for childhood disorders. But it is a risk factor we can greatly reduce by raising awareness of its pernicious effects. Parental stress, whether in the womb or postnatally, can affect the child to a small degree, such as frequent stomach-aches, *or* to a larger degree, such as ADHD, autism or asthma. In this chapter, we will examine the effects of parental stress after a child is born.

In Chapter 5 we saw that, while in the womb, the PAR gets its information from, among other things, the level of stress hormones *in utero*. But here is the key concept of this chapter: once the child is born, the PAR appears to get its information from **attunement** with parents, since kids pick up on everything—especially stress.

The postnatal research linking parental stress to immune disorders is compelling. For two years, Dr. Peter Wyman and his team monitored the stress levels and frequency of child illness in 169 families treated at the Pediatrics Department of the University of Rochester. Parents filled out surveys about any stressors or mental illness they had, and their children's blood was tested for levels of NK (natural killer) cells, which are part of the immune response to illness.

Results showed that children with stressed parents had 11 percent more general illnesses, 36 percent more illnesses with fever, and carried around 15 percent more immune response cells in their bloodstreams than children of non-stressed parents. Dr. Wyman concludes that stressful households are linked to increased immune response illnesses in children.

Other research supports that conclusion. In 2004 Dr. Rosalind Wright of Harvard studied 114 families, measuring the stress levels of the parents at two-month intervals during the first two years of their babies' lives. Once the babies turned two, she tested their blood to see if they had elevated levels of immunity-related cells, which is a sign they will develop allergies or asthma. She found that the children of parents with high stress levels were more than twice as likely to develop asthma or allergies as other children.

There is research linking parental stress to other immune disorders, including arthritis and diabetes. Dr. Michael Von Korff is a Senior Investigator at the Center for Health Studies in Seattle. At first, his focus was on the mental health disorders of patients at community health clinics. Most common were depression and anxiety disorders. But Dr. Von Korff also became fascinated because many depressed or anxious patients also complained of chronic pain. Perhaps there was some kind of mind-body connection between the two?

When members of the World Mental Health Survey asked him to join their team, Dr. Von Korff was given access to data that many others had ignored in the past, like what kind of adversities adults with chronic conditions had suffered when they were children, and how old they were at first onset of their chronic conditions.

Dr. Von Korff went on to publish the results of an astounding 18,000 cases he analyzed. He concluded that childhood stressors were a significant risk factor for chronic illness later in life, including arthritis, diabetes, chronic pain and asthma.

It may seem surprising that stressed-out families seem to play a role even in Type 1 diabetes, but researchers in Sweden demonstrated this occurs even in children whose families have no history of diabetes, according to a study of 4,400 families, done at Sweden's top-ranked medical school.

The parents of these 4,400 kids filled out forms measuring their level of personal and relationship stress when their child was a newborn and again at one year of age. The scientists also took blood samples from the children at birth and at age one, to see whether certain antibodies associated with diabetes were unusually high.

The experts found that high stress in the parents increased the risk of diabetes-related antibodies in the children's bloodstream by 80 percent, and a family's stressful life events increased the children's diabetes risk by 230 percent. Surprisingly, these results remained the same regardless of whether there was any history of diabetes in the family.

The authors concluded that children soak up the stress in a household, which affects their brain's stress response. This has a cascade effect, increasing certain hormones which impact the immune system—specifically, insulin sensitivity and insulin need.

Household stress can greatly increase the risk of children developing immune disorders in their first years of life. A key question is how? After a child is born, how does so much parental stress get transferred to the child via attunement? A child cannot simply sit in the same room with his parents and psychically soak up their stress. Rather, many stressed-out parents have a typical behavior—a typical way of (unknowingly) passing their stress onto their child. That behavior is known as Vulnerable Child Syndrome. Let's take a look at a real-life example:

A Typical Example of How a Child Soaks Up Parental Stress

Alexis and her husband Zach were facing financial challenges. Zach didn't get the bonus they were expecting, and they were falling behind on their mortgage payments. Every time they tried to discuss the issue, however, it escalated into an argument. As a result, they began to distance emotionally from each other. Zach spent more time at the office, and Alexis paid more attention—perhaps even too much attention—to the kids. When the couple was together, they stuck to banal topics and avoided bringing up touchy issues—especially money. But unresolved tension pervaded the house, and Alexis started having trouble sleeping.

One night when she was lying awake, she heard her three-year-old son Eric cough in his sleep. Alexis had already been concerned that perhaps he had asthma or allergies, so when she heard him cough, her anxiety really spiked.

She decided this cough must be serious, and some action needed to be taken. Alexis got up, woke Eric, gave him cough medicine, went back to bed, and fell asleep almost immediately.

The next morning, as usual, things were tense between Alexis and her husband as he headed out the door to work. Alexis was sitting in the kitchen, alone and upset, when her son came downstairs and coughed again. This time, she picked up the phone and made an appointment with the pediatrician.

The pediatrician's examination was inconclusive. Eric might have allergies, he said, or perhaps just a virus. He also noted that Eric hadn't awakened from his cough the night before, or even complained about it. But Alexis wanted to play it safe, so she persuaded the doctor to prescribe an asthma inhaler for her son. After all, it was spring, and other mothers had told her how they sent their kids to school with inhalers every day, just to be safe. Who knew how bad the dust and pollen counts might get?

Alexis and Zach's example is typical of how parental stress may harm a child's health after the child is born. Parents may be exacerbating health problems through *child focus*. Child focus is a form of helicopter parenting where hovering parents anxiously focus on their child's symptom, sometimes blowing it out of proportion and thereby exacerbating it.

In Eric's case, the real problem lies in the parents' marriage, and Alexis's heightened stress levels. But it becomes Eric's problem because his attunement allows him to "catch" his parents' stress like a contagious virus, as we discussed in Chapter 3. As a result, a child with unconfirmed symptoms of mild allergies may fall victim to child focus, and his mild cough turns him into the "identified patient" on which the family focuses—a kind of "designated symptom-bearer" of the family's anxiety.

We have now arrived at a key juncture in this book. Let's take a breath and review where we have been before we proceed further:

- Chapter 1 gave an overview of parental stress as a risk factor to children's health;
- Chapter 2 explained how a parent's stress hormones pass to a child in the womb;
- Chapter 3 discussed how, after birth, a parent's stress continues to pass to a child via attunement;
- Chapter 4 taught how stress switches some genes on or off through epigenetics;
- Chapter 5 explained how an evolutionary process called the Predictive Adaptive Response is triggered by stress hormones in the womb to switch certain genes on or off in the fetal brain;
- Chapter 6 will now teach how the PAR continues to direct the development in a child's brain even after it is born. Obviously,

the stress hormones impacting the PAR no longer come from the womb. Rather, the attunement between parent and child, as discussed in Chapter 2, is the PRINCIPAL route by which kids pick up on everything outside the womb.

However, since in Chapter 2 we have already discussed attunement as the primary mechanism by which kids pick up on everything, we will not dwell on attunement again. Rather, let me simply repeat that attunement is the key concept to remember here. However, there is also another way by which parental stress is passed on to children. It is not as primary as attunement, but it is very important. It is called Vulnerable Child Syndrome.

Vulnerable Child Syndrome

Medical research describes this intense child-focus as *Vulnerable Child Syndrome*. VCS was first named as a medical issue in 1964 when more and more doctors noted that anxious parents of a child who had a brush with death begin to over-parent that child, leading to a higher incidence of social and even physical symptoms. Like attunement, VCS is a two-way street between parent and child: first the child picks up on the parent's stress via attunement, and this stress exacerbates the child's symptoms. Then the parent picks up on the child's increased stress and suffering via attunement, and overreacts to that because the parent already has heightened stress levels. This back-and-forth overreaction escalates until finally the child develops a serious, tangible, diagnosable symptom and the parent becomes completely obsessed with it.

There is a growing consensus that some of today's parents over-parent their kids even without a crisis. An anxious, hovering parent may be predisposed to transforming any defect in the child from a molehill into a mountain. These parents don't realize they're projecting their anxiety onto their child, so when they seek a "diagnosis" they create a self-fulfilling prophecy.

Modern psychology explains this "off-loading anxiety" phenomenon in terms of "binding anxiety in the identified patient." It's as if the family's cloud of free-floating anxiety comes to rest over one child and rains constantly upon him or her. The family remarks on how the child is "wet" without realizing they helped make it rain on him or her.

Midwives have noted this phenomenon for centuries, where most families tend to have only one sickly child. The sickly child becomes a kind of unconscious scapegoat or "whipping boy" for the anxiety of the household.

Although VCS can exacerbate any symptom in a child, it has become particularly common among families struggling with allergies or asthma. In 2001, Susan Dominus reported in the *New York Times Magazine* how some anxious parents blow their children's symptoms out of proportion, contributing to a diagnosis of allergies that may or may not be accurate. Dominus quotes Dr. Hugh Sampson, chief of the division of pediatric allergy and immunology at Mount Sinai Medical Center: "Hypochondria is a big problem in this area…. There's definitely a certain personality type." Sampson describes certain parents who seem to have a strange fixation on their children's alleged food allergies, treating these allergies as self-evident even in the absence of evidence.

Dr. Michael Welch sees this phenomena all the time. He is co-director of the Allergy and Asthma Medical Group and Research Center at the University of California, San Diego, School of Medicine. He thinks parental anxiety levels are on the rise in developed nations, and he observes this anxiety on a daily basis, especially in the context of food allergy:

> *The stories that come up more than ever are the ones related to food allergy. The problem of food allergy has become immense - there has been an "epidemic" of children developing food allergy, like peanut allergy. It seems to be affecting educated, upper middle class parents to a greater extent than other SES classes…. Parents of these children, who are often very successful, and are used to being in control of their personal lives and careers, have a child, and are "dealt" a food allergy problem, which has no cure. Certain types of food allergy, like peanut and tree nut allergy, can indeed be life-threatening. The only approach at this time for a serious food allergy, is for the parent to make sure the child avoids the food. Carrying out food avoidance can be pretty easy when the child is a toddler - but, as the child grows older, it becomes harder. The child enters*

school, and is no longer completely under the wing of the parent. Certain
parents, who have a need to be in complete control, and who accept only
a 0% risk their child will be exposed accidentally to the food they are
allergic to, have a lot of difficulty with how accommodating the school
is of their child's food allergy. I have had parents asking schools to carry
out extreme and unreasonable measures to make sure their allergic child is
safe at school.

As a result of this parental fear, I have seen children become so afraid
of exposure to their allergic food at school, that they refuse to even go to
school. It becomes a school phobia. Only with the help of a psychologist
has the child made it back to school. [from an email to author]

Dr. Welch is using food allergy as an example to describe a trend of growing anxiety in households across the country. A recent massive study of over two million doctor visits shows that food allergies in children lead to more severe allergic diseases that affect up to 50 million Americans, including asthma, which now affects one in ten children.

Today's trend of increased child immune disorders seems unlikely to be due to increased exposure to toxic substances or to genetic inheritance. At the Centre for Health Policy in Winnipeg, Canada, Dr. Anita Kozyrskyj scoured the health care and prescription records of almost 14,000 families to find all mothers who had sought medication for anxiety. She found that children of these anxious mothers were 25 percent more likely to develop asthma by age seven, even after she factored out other well-known factors that contribute to asthma. But most surprising was her discovery that the risk actually *increased* in high-income households, where children of anxious mothers were a whopping 44 percent more likely to develop asthma.

This study serves as excellent evidence for the role of parental anxiety and worry in exacerbating symptoms. It found that, if mothers were able to reduce their anxiety in the first year of their child's lives, the increased risk factor of asthma went away. This suggests the children may have picked up their mother's anxiety *in utero*, which triggered their predictive adaptive response and created asthma symptoms when the baby was a newborn. However, those moms who could reduce their anxiety in that first year had the "Dr. Meaney" effect on their children, as if they had licked them like the calm mother rats, discussed in Chapter 4. The mothers' reduced anxiety had the effect of calming the children down, and that's why the newborns' asthma symptoms went away. But for those children whose mothers didn't calm down in the first year, it could be Vulnerable Child Syndrome that exacerbated the symptoms.

Today's doctors privately lament the number of anxious parents who bring in kids with health symptoms created by both the parent and the child playing off each other. But it's easier to write a prescription than persuade parents that their anxiety actually contributes to their child's poor health. Doctors I've interviewed say they would rather keep their office visits short than play shrink and risk a confrontation. And some parents would rather give their kid a pill than face how they're projecting their own insecurities onto their children. But top pediatricians privately acknowledge that anxious parenting contributes to the severity of symptoms a child develops.

It is important to note that in many cases children DO need help and treatment, and of course parents should seek professional advice if they have any doubts about their kids' development. But sometimes it's hard to tell which disorders were already present in a child because of prenatal programming, and which disorders were created in part by a combination of attunement and Vulnerable Child Syndrome.

Vulnerable Child Syndrome Linked to Neuro Disorders like ADHD

The above examples portray how VCS can exacerbate immune response disorders in a young child. But the same back-and-forth escalation can also take place between children with neurodevelopmental disorders and their parents.

You may recall from Chapter 5 that Harvard's National Scientific Council for the Developing Child describes how parental stress has been "linked to alterations in the stress response and immune systems of the fetus." But the Council goes on to describe how any symptoms created prenatally can "increase the chance that an infant will be more vulnerable to irritable, intrusive, or withdrawn maternal care than the average baby. (Paper #8, Pg 7)" Our focus here is specifically on "intrusive maternal care," in the context of helicopter parents anxiously hovering over their child or obsessively monitoring for any symptoms of a problem, as in Vulnerable Child Syndrome.

In the case of neurodevelopmental disorders, let's say that, by the time the child is born, he or she may already be predisposed to an oversensitive stress response that is too easily triggered, and this makes the child chronically overreactive to the parent's emotions via the "emotional pipeline" of their attunement, as discussed in Chapter 3.

Several studies suggest that this hypersensitivity to stress predisposes young children to resist their parents' communications. The child may react badly to any irritability or indifference shown by the parent. This renders the child impulsive, or overreactive. He or she therefore acts out or gets into arguments or tantrums easily. In mild neurological cases like ADHD, the child was not necessarily born with a behavior disorder, but the overreactive parental behavior bounced off the overreactive child behavior, back and forth, until the escalation of reactivity may lead to disruptions outside the home as well.

Teachers, school counselors, and clergy tell me they are constantly amazed at the unprecedented level of disorders in today's children. The National Scientific Council states, "Public awareness of significant emotional and behavioral problems in early childhood is growing, as preschool teachers report increasingly major disruptions in their classrooms and kindergarten teachers identify social and emotional problems as a common impediment to school readiness (Page 3)."

An anxious parent can contribute to this back-and-forth escalation by overreacting to her child's impulsive behavior and creating a self-fulfilling prophecy that ends up diagnosed as ADHD. The prominent neuroscientist Jaak Panksepp believes we parents now overreact to what used to be a normal activity: rough-and-tumble play.

According to Dr. Panksepp, rough-and-tumble play used to fall within the range of normal behavior, but somewhere along the line it became pathologized as part of a diagnosis of attention deficit/hyperactivity disorder. Dr. Panksepp suggests that the behavior of children didn't change so much as did parents' and teachers' unwillingness to tolerate it. In the past, kids who squirmed in their seats and didn't pay attention got all their impulsiveness out on the playground during recess. Today, a dramatic number of kids, especially boys, are often forced to take medications. Dr. Panksepp expresses concern about this trend:

> *Are excessively playful children now being medicated to reduce their natural desire to play, on the pretext that they have some type of impulse-control disorder? This seems to be the case for at least some of the children who are being medicated. If so, it is unconscionable to give them anti-play drugs such as methylphenidate instead of providing substantial opportunities for rough-and-tumble play at the appropriate times of day, such as early in the morning when such urges are especially high. Even more frightening is the fact that the nervous system becomes sensitized to psychostimulants, and animal research indicates that such modifications of the nervous system can be permanent. Are we now permanently altering the nervous systems of children with psychostimulant medications? Might we not actually be retarding the natural growth of the brain by reducing the normal influence of playful behaviors on central nervous system development?*

Disciplining an unruly child is one thing, but giving him medication to squelch what used to be normal behavior is another. Medications for ADHD have become routine treatment, but Panksepp draws a distinction between what's common and what's normal. It may have become common to give a child medication, but there's nothing normal about permanently altering his brain development.

Such helicopter parenting simply wasn't possible in the past when four or more kids were the norm and moms—who lacked modern "conveniences" like washing machines and grocery stores—were much busier simply keeping their families alive and fed. And yet in today's frenzy of

Vulnerable Child Syndrome, we accept such drastic medications with hardly a shudder.

When Parents Love Too Much

It is important to know that, with Vulnerable Child Syndrome, there are often two interrelated factors that worsen the child's symptoms. One is the child-focus described above, with anxious parents hovering over the child's every move. Another is *enmeshment*, where a mother who may throw herself into caring for her "troubled" child, to the detriment of both her child and herself.

UCSD's Dr. Michael Welch explains enmeshment this way:

[When] the child becomes the parent's best friend, issues of enmeshment between the child and parent are common in all chronic diseases, including asthma. The parent begins to 'own' the child's disease, and the parent and the patient become inseparable. The tip-off for this, is when the parent, in talking about the child's symptoms or problems since the last office visit, will use the word 'we' instead of 'he' or 'she.' I then know I need to work with the parent to make sure they understand that they are not 'one-and-the-same' with their child. [from an email to author]

As we will discuss in great detail in Part 2, a pregnant woman with a troubled marriage or family problems may feel tremendously isolated and stressed. But once that child is born, she has a brand-new relationship that can eclipse all other relationships.

Every mother knows that the mother-infant bond can be incredibly powerful and all-consuming. Breastfeeding alone releases all kinds of bonding hormones. If the mother had problems with her spouse or parents, they are suddenly dwarfed as she throws herself into her new relationship with her first baby. Compared to her relationship with her husband, her relationship with her baby may seem perfect. Her baby doesn't argue with her or reject her. Her baby needs her, and she may love to feel needed. And especially if her baby has health problems, the mother's all-consuming sacrifices for her child's welfare may be a welcome relief from the relationship with her husband. Now she has the perfect excuse to avoid any problems in her marriage.

The famous child pediatrician Dr. T. Berry Brazelton, writes, "The problem with an 'over-mothered' child is well known in pediatrics, where it is sometimes called the 'Vulnerable Child Syndrome.' Overprotection affects the child's image of himself, leaving him to feel that he always needs to be protected, and that he is unable to take care of himself. …We see this in mothers who are having a lonely, tough time themselves."

In this pattern of intrusive parenting, it's no accident that the parent becomes the child's best friend. Usually, the symptom-bearing child becomes an escape for the mother from her unfulfilling marriage. And that's the problem. Many parents believe that the more attention they give their kids, the better they'll turn out. But there is such a thing as too much.

In the name of love, we may intervene too often in our child's welfare. Our children are precious gifts, and of course we would do anything for them—*except* hamper their ability to stand on their own two feet. Psychiatrist Carl Jung believed that the greatest detriment to children was the unlived life of their parents. When the tension goes up in our marriages, we may subconsciously escape by focusing on someone else around us, often our kids. The *New York Times* family columnist and author Judith Warner writes:

> *Studies have never shown that total immersion in motherhood makes mothers happy or does their children any good. On the contrary, studies have shown that mothers who are able to make a life for themselves tend to be happy and to make their children happy. The self-fulfillment they get from a well-rounded life actually makes them more emotionally available for their children—in part because they're less needy…. [However,] we manage not to acknowledge, despite endless clues from our children's doctors and teachers, that our preferred parenting style [i.e., helicopter-style] is not terribly conducive to promoting future happiness. We persist in doing things that are contrary to our best interests—and our children's best interests. And we continue, against all logic, to subscribe to a way of thinking about motherhood that leaves us guilt-ridden, anxious, and exhausted.*

It's time for us to question the status quo, because the status quo is not working. Many of us have come to take for granted that total immersion parenting raises happier kids. And yet, as we look around at our family and friends, where is the evidence? How can all the anxiety, guilt, and fatigue caused by today's helicopter parenting yield happier kids if the parents are increasingly isolated and unhappy themselves? We need to face the fact that the emperor has no clothes—today's children and their parents are suffering more, not less, despite all our frenetic investment of time and attention.

We parents already have a lot of guilt, and we feel pressure to "get it right." In drawing a link between helicopter parenting and Vulnerable Child Syndrome, my goal is not to add more guilt. Rather, I'm trying to provide a way of looking at the problem that could be liberating, because if we can get to the root of the cause, we can begin to fix it. We need to address the cause, rather than getting caught up in all the symptoms.

At first, it's painful to think we might have been hurting a loved one without realizing it. But it's short-term pain for long-term gain. There's no need to beat ourselves up—we didn't know we were doing it. And the long-term gain is that we can nip our child-focus in the bud before it has any more ill effects on our children. That's good news for you and your family. Our families are truly worth the struggle—they are, after all, where much of our happiness in this world resides.

To sum up this section: yes, parental stress can create child disorders prenatally, but intrusive parenting with an intense child-focus like VCS can whip the flames much higher, by further programming the child's stress response to easily overload and overreact. The Harvard National Scientific Council for the Developing Child states that "stress-system overload can significantly diminish a child's ability to learn and engage in typical social interactions across the lifespan."

It's time parents became aware of this vicious circle: Overreactive parents tend to have overreactive children, whose behaviors then make their parents even more overreactive. It's a primal, instinctive process that takes place beneath our awareness.

Now that we've looked at how stress affects a child's health in both the prenatal and postnatal stages, let's address some of the skepticism that may emerge regarding this topic.

An Important FAQ For Parents

As you read this book, you may be thinking, "My second pregnancy was actually more stressful than my first, so why does my first-born have more problems?"

Any mother with more than one child can compare pregnancies and tell you which one seemed more stressful. In a family with multiple kids, one would expect the most stressful pregnancy to yield the child with the most symptoms, but this often seems not to be the case. Sugey Cruz Everts from Texas, the mother of a child with ASD, puts it this way:

> *There are so many cases now that I can think of, where friends have multiple children, and only their oldest [child] has autism, and their younger kids do not... Wouldn't the parent be even more stressed with the birth of a new child after knowing that their first child has autism? Why is the second child fine then?*

I can think of two other possible explanations for why the first-born child is more likely to have problems, even if a mother's second pregnancy seemed more stressful:

- First, with a woman's first pregnancy comes a dramatic change of lifestyle, coupled with fear of the unknown about child rearing, as well as the anxiety about the pain of delivery. All of that may produce much more stress than we think;
- Second, a child's disorder develops not only in the womb. As discussed in this chapter, a parent's child-focus and enmeshment may contribute to the severity of a child's symptoms.

Let's look at my first response—fear of the unknown is a significant factor in first pregnancies, and first-time mothers may be more stressed than they realize. Researchers in Italy and England have noted higher stress levels in women who are pregnant for the first time:

There is preliminary evidence in animals and in humans, that the novel experience of the first pregnancy could raise the level of apprehension in primigravid [pregnant for the first time] women Specifically, circadian cortisol [i.e. stress hormone] secretion pattern appears to be distinctive in primiparous [pregnant for the first time] women [which] could modify maternal glucocorticoids levels [i.e., stress-hormones] and affect fetal development [i.e., the PAR and epigenetics].

Motherhood is one of the greatest gifts (and challenges) known to humans. Along with a woman's joy at her first pregnancy, she may harbor all kinds of self-doubt, both conscious and unconscious, as to whether she can handle motherhood. And as we will discuss in the next chapter, if one adds to this a troubled marriage or problems with her parents or in-laws, then relationship stress and isolation may accentuate her fears of the unknown, and produce plenty of stress hormones crossing her placenta.

The second reason that more first-borns have problems than subsequent children may have to do with enmeshment and VCS.

Regarding enmeshment, research suggests that, after a baby is born, many "feel-good" hormones such as oxytocin and vasopressin are released, which reduce a mother's stress levels. Furthermore, the mother-infant bond with her first child lowers her stress levels, since if a mother has troubled, stressful relationships, then the enmeshment with her first baby can fulfill her relationship needs. These lowered stress levels may offer a hidden "blessing" to the second child in her womb, exposing him or her to lower levels of stress hormones. Fewer stress hormones *in utero* mean the PAR will form a less-overreactive stress response for that second fetus.

Although research on this area of first pregnancies is limited, it suggests that women pregnant with their first child (and with marriage problems) would have relatively high levels of stress hormones in their wombs, due to fear of the unknown and troubled relationships. These women would have lower levels of stress hormones in subsequent pregnancies, because their first baby fulfilled so many relationship needs and triggered so many positive, bonding hormones. Future studies will give us a more detailed understanding of this state and hopefully help us identify effective interventions.

Regarding Vulnerable Child Syndrome, a first-born can have problems that his or her younger siblings do not because the troubled child becomes the identified patient of the family, attracting the anxiety of the parents like a magnet. You may recall earlier in this chapter our discussion of child-focus, where one child develops a symptom, and the stressed parent then overreacts to the symptoms and treats the child specially. This may make the sickly child the center of attention in the family, thus creating a self-fulfilling prophecy. That's why, in a stressed family, not every child develops a serious ailment—usually only one does, as psychiatrist Dr. Michael Kerr of Georgetown Family Center explained in his article, "Why Do Siblings Turn Out Differently?"

To sum up, parental stress is a risk factor prenatally because parental stress hormones cross the placenta and trigger the predictive adaptive response in the womb. But the predictive adaptive response continues to influence a child's genes even after the child has left the womb. Kids continue to pick up on everything via attunement primarily, but also because of Vulnerable Child Syndrome. In both the prenatal and postnatal stages, parental stress is a risk factor for both neurodevelopmental disorders and immune-disorders, as well as other disorders like obesity.

The more parental stress, the more likely the child will develop a more serious disorder, but even mild disorders appear to share parental stress as a risk factor. And even if a child is born with a relatively mild disorder, attunement and VCS can fan the flames into something much bigger.

So, Where is All This Stress Coming From?

We have now examined compelling evidence that parental stress affects a child's health. Chapter 2 looked at that process inside the womb, and Chapter 3 covered attunement and the mind-body connection after a child is born. Chapter 4 explained epigenetics, the most likely mechanism by which stress affects a child's body, and Chapter 5 explained how the predictive adaptive response is a factor in problems from neurodevelopmental disorders such as ADHD and ASD to immune disorders such as allergies and asthma.

The remaining question is, Why now? Why would today's parents be more stressed-out than in the past, and why would parental stress be causing such harm to today's children? We'll address these questions in Part 2.

PART TWO

The Mother is Not to Blame: Why Did Stress Become a Risk Factor NOW?

If stress is a risk factor in children's health, especially prenatally, why is the mother not to blame?

As we will examine in detail in this section, the mother is not to blame because there are two social trends at the root of today's rising anxiety in society.

1) The first trend is increasing isolation. Humans have forgotten we are social animals with a primal need to socialize and to fit in. As we socialize less, our stress levels go up;

2) Our increasing stress levels lead to the second trend: we now spend more time in primal, flight-response every day, although we are not aware of it. This plays havoc with our marriages, and our kids are picking up on the increased tension in our households.

There has always been stress. Why would it be a risk factor NOW?

You may ask why stress would be such a major factor for children's health now, of all times. After all, stress is nothing new, so why the sudden epidemic of stress-related disorders? I have been corresponding with Elizabeth Verdick, the mother of an autistic child named Zach in Saint Paul, Minn. I quote her below because she articulates a good question:

> *If prenatal stress is linked to autism and other health issues (like asthma and allergies), then why is there a greater prevalence today than in the past? Throughout history, pregnant women have endured war, poverty, illness, loss, grief, lack of rights, lack of adequate medical care, and every imaginable stressor—and most didn't bear children with ASD [Autism Spectrum Disorder]. Many of us today have greater resources and better access to healthcare and education (compared to women of times past), and yet our children frequently experience the health issues discussed here. I can't look back with confidence and say my pregnancy was particularly stressful...any pregnancy is stressful because of body changes, concern for the health of the child, and added responsibilities. Not all of that stress is bad.*

To respond to Elizabeth's question, I do not claim that ASD is all about stress only—stress is only one of several risk factors, and genetics is definitely another risk factor. But Part 2 will offer several answers to Elizabeth's excellent question. Bottom line: Today's stress is a contributing factor to the epidemic of children's ailments because we simply didn't notice that we have gradually become more isolated and stressed, nor did we realize all the health consequences for our families.

In Part 2, we will discuss how so much stress has shown up in today's families. The following chapters will address several points:

7) Our Dwindling Social Networks Leave Parents More Stressed Than Ever
8) Today's Parents Have Gone Primal, in Constant Fight-or-Flight Mode
9) Your Marriage May Be Much More Stressful Than You Think
10) Your Marriage Affects Your Child More Than You Think
11) Myth: The More Attention We Give Our Kids, the Better They Turn Out

Chapter 7

Our Dwindling Social Networks Leave Parents More Stressed Than Ever

In his critically-acclaimed book, *Outliers*, Malcolm Gladwell tells the story of the University of Oklahoma Medical School professor, Stewart Wolf. In the late 1950's, Dr. Wolf discovered a small town in Pennsylvania, Roseto, that was freakishly healthy: the death rate was roughly 35 percent lower than the national average for people under 65, and there was virtually no crime, drug addiction, suicide, or even peptic ulcers.

Dr. Wolf started looking for reasons for the Rosetans' success by analyzing their diet, but he found they cooked with lard and ate more sweets then typical. More than 40 percent of their daily caloric intake was from fat; they struggled with obesity, and smoked heavily.

Dr. Wolf then searched out cousins of the Rosetans who lived elsewhere, to see if they were equally as healthy as their relatives in Pennsylvania. They were not, so Dr. Wolf ruled out genetics. He also noted that in towns neighboring Roseto, the death rate from heart disease was three times higher, so he ruled out location as a factor.

It was when Dr. Wolf invited a sociologist to join his research that they finally discovered why Roseto was so healthy:

They looked at how the Rosetans visited each other, stopping to chat with each other in Italian on the street, or cooking for each other in their backyards. They learned about the extended family clans that underlay the town's social structure. They saw how many homes had three generations living under one roof, and how much respect grandparents commanded...They counted twenty-two separate civic organizations in a town of just under 2000 people. They picked up on the particular egalitarian ethos of the town, that discouraged the wealthy from flaunting their success and helped the unsuccessful obscure their failures...the Rosetans had created a powerful, protective social structure capable of insulating them from the pressures of the modern world.

Nobody is claiming we should return to the 1950's, because there were plenty of problems in society then. But we may have forgotten one valuable aspect of that era—socializing.

In this chapter, we will learn how our dwindling social support networks have left us all more stressed. We'll address three main points:

- Humans are social animals, and socializing gives us a sense of well-being. The less we socialize, the more anxious and stressed-out we become;
- We don't realize we are caught in a vicious circle: our increasing isolation makes us more stressed and irritable, which leads to ever-more isolation;
- We don't realize how stressed we are. We are living in denial.

Humans Are Social Animals

The story of Roseto reminds us that *Homo sapiens* is a herd animal—"social to the core," as the best-selling author and primatologist Frans de Waal puts it. Like other herd animals, we also have a primal need to bond. Our primate cousins bond with each other through grooming, and humans need face-time with friends and family to bond and satisfy the social needs at the core of our being, as research confirms.

Martin Seligman is a psychology professor at University of Pennsylvania and former president of the American Psychological

Association. He writes that there is an epidemic of depression today because there is "something about modern life that creates fertile soil for depression." Dr. Seligman notes the absence of depression in highly social communities like the Kaluli tribes of New Guinea and the Amish of Pennsylvania.

As Americans play less, socialize less, and have sex less, it's no surprise that our anxiety, insomnia and health problems increase. But there's also another, hidden cost. Today's crisis in child disorders may be linked to increased stress, because of our reduced social bonding and dwindling social-support networks. This crisis may touch almost every family. We don't realize how stressed-out we have become, and researchers in various other institutes have come to the same conclusion. Dr. Twenge of San Diego State University writes:

> *Many social statistics point to a breakdown in social connectedness. The divorce rate has increased, the birth rate has dropped, people marry later in life, and many more people now live alone (11% in 1950, compared with 25% in 1997). In addition, Putnam (2000) found that Americans are now less likely to join community organizations and visit friends than they once were. Connectedness can also be measured by levels of trust (Fukuyama, 1999), and these levels have also declined (only 18.3% of high school seniors in 1992 agreed that you can usually trust people, compared with 34.5% in 1975; Smith, 1997).*

Remember in the 1990s, when the media coined the term "cocooning" to describe a trend where people were socializing less and retreating to their homes more? We never hear about cocooning anymore, but that's not because it went away. It simply became the norm, so it's no longer newsworthy. Dr. Twenge notes that the increase in anxiety in the past 50 years has been so large that, "The average American child in the 1980s reported more anxiety than child psychiatric patients in the 1950s. Correlations with social indices (e.g., divorce rates, crime rates) suggest that decreases in social connectedness and increases in environmental dangers may be responsible for the rise in anxiety…Societies with low levels of social integration produce adults prone to anxiety." (pg. 1018)

We Are Caught in a Vicious Circle of Increasing Stress and Isolation

At University of Southern California Medical School, Dr. Joel Milam observes on a daily basis how low social integration produces anxious adults who, in turn, produce children with disorders. Since childhood, Dr. Milam has had allergies that he noticed were exacerbated by stress, sparking his interest in the mind-body connection between stress and respiratory health.

Dr. Milam is also the proud father of 6-year-old twins and a 9-month-old baby, which led him to an unexpected discovery. When USC was putting together a study of thousands of kids with respiratory issues, most of his colleagues were focused on toxic substances and allergens. But Dr. Milam was thinking about stress. He knew the medical literature linked prenatal stress to low birth weight, and low birth weight was a risk factor for asthma.

But his colleagues looked at him like he was from Mars when he requested that questions about the mothers' anxiety levels be included in the surveys that USC was handing out to these thousands of families. "We fought hard to get the stress items on this large cohort study of thousands of kids," Dr. Milam recalls. "I was surprised how hard it was."

What the USC team found was that children in mildly-stressed families were 18 percent more likely to develop an asthmatic wheeze, but children (especially boys) in highly-stressed families were almost three times more likely to develop asthma than children of non-stressed families.

Amazingly, these results held true even among children with *no parental history of asthma whatsoever*.

When I asked Dr. Milam how he explained these findings, he said there is a growing amount of research demonstrating that anxiety and depression are increasing in the U.S. He believes the increase is too big to be explained away as simply better diagnosis. He agrees with the argument in Robert Putnam's book, *Bowling Alone*, explaining, "People don't live where they grew up anymore. Given how transient we are these days, there are no longer multiple generations living in the same home or neighborhood. There is a large body of medical literature for social support and its relationship to health."

In other words, we don't realize that we are becoming increasingly isolated, and isolation is driving our increased anxiety, which affects our health more than we thought. Again, Dr. Twenge:

> *Over the last few decades, people seem to have become more anxious, worrying about safety, social acceptance, and job security more than in the past (e.g., Rosen, 1998; Sloan, 1996). The perceived trend is so strong that some authors have labeled the twentieth century 'the age of anxiety' (e.g., Spielberger & Rickman, 1990 p. 69). These descriptions imply that modern life produces higher levels of anxiety.*

Drs. Milam and Twenge point out to the mounting evidence that our decreased social grooming has increased our anxiety, and recently it has hit critical mass in a vicious circle:

- With less social-grooming comes increased anxiety;
- Increased anxiety makes us more irritable and triggers our fight-or-flight response more often;
- To fight with others further increases our stress, or else our flight response from others increases our isolation;
- Conflict, isolation and lack of social grooming increase our stress;
- …and so on, in an increasingly vicious circle.

Outside America, most other cultures still recognize that visiting with one another is the "social grooming" that maintains mental health. When we travel abroad, we can see how much more certain cultures socialize. In many cultures, for example, people show up at all hours of the day or night unannounced on their cousin's, neighbor's or friend's doorstep. The town square is still the center of social life in some countries; families visit with their friends and relatives in the village square each evening, while their kids play together nearby. And we downright envy the cafe culture of Europeans, who linger over coffee and meals. In countries where three generations of a family often live in close proximity, rates of divorce and addictions are lower, and people seem happier.

Other nations may envy our wealth, but they don't envy our social lives or our troubled families. A review by scientists at Cornell University of several large scientific studies confirmed a trend of increasing isolation and depression in the U.S., Sweden, Germany, Canada, and New Zealand. Perhaps most compelling was the finding that, in very social communities like Puerto Rico and Mexican-American neighborhoods in the U.S., there was no trend toward anxiety or depression.

Americans' isolation is rapidly increasing as we lead a more transient lifestyle, and "groom" each other less and less. We visit our parents less often, drift away from our relatives, move away from our friends, and distance ourselves emotionally from our spouses. Our focus on our children and our schedules leaves us short on sleep, sex, and any sense of fun or belonging to a community. And the size of our communities has changed, such that now, most of us live in immense cities. You have no choice but to be part of a community when your town is tiny, but it's all too easy to be without community in a huge city. Creating a community takes work.

The number of respondents to the 2005 General Social Survey saying they have no one to confide in has tripled since the 1985 survey. Over the same 20 years, the average American went from having about three confidants with whom they discuss important matters to only two confidants. Authors of the study acknowledge "these shrinking networks reflect an important social change in America."

Dr. Twenge also describes a growing sense of alienation among Americans, asserting, "as American culture shifted toward emphasizing individual achievement, money, and status rather than social relationships and community, psychopathology increased among young people."

Most people mistakenly assume that being too busy is their primary source of stress. We need to wake up to relationships as the primary source. Humans are social animals on a primal level. Our main source of stress is our relationships, or the lack thereof. Those folks who watch Discovery

Channel have seen how vulnerable and stressed an animal becomes when ostracized from its herd. And most people have noticed that those who become increasingly isolated also become increasingly stressed. Humans need social interaction to assure them they fit in and are still part of the group. From socially-awkward kids sitting alone in the cafeteria to campus shooters or the Unabomber, increasing isolation usually spells trouble.

We humans are kidding ourselves that we are individual beings, rather than social animals who live in a web of relationships. Our social support networks are the key determinant of our stress levels and mental health. For example, if we have conflict with our parents, siblings or relatives, that is obviously a stressor. Conversely, if we "keep the peace" by distancing emotionally from our families of origin, the resulting lack of social support also raises our stress levels. Isolation breeds anxiety, although we may not be consciously aware of this effect.

In his book, *Social Intelligence: The New Science Of Human Relationships*, Daniel Goleman makes the case for social support networks when he describes this link between a child's relationships and the epigenetics of the child's developing brain:

> *Now epigenetic studies are looking at how parents treat a growing child, finding ways child rearing shapes that child's brain. A child's brain comes preprogrammed to grow, but it takes a bit more than the first two decades of life to finish this task, making it the last organ of the body to become anatomically mature. Over that period all the major figures in a child's life—parents, siblings, grandparents, teachers, and friends—can become active ingredients in brain growth, creating a social and emotional mix that drives neural development. Like a plant adapting to rich or to depleted soil, a child's brain shapes itself to fit its social ecology, particularly the emotional climate fostered by the main people in her life (p. 152).*

In other words, it does take at least a tribe, if not a village, to raise a child. "Social support network" is just a fancy word for the tribal structure that used to provide *Homo sapiens* with the social support and nurture we need to thrive.

So it should be no surprise that, over the past 20 years, as parents socialize less with their own parents, spouses, and friends, our increasing isolation ratchets up our stress and anxiety. Consider how Jennifer Hutchings of Northern California, the mother of an autistic child, describes how her pregnancy was affected by estrangement from her mother:

My sister, aunt, and grandmother came to my baby shower and I remember the uncomfortable looks on their faces when I asked, "Where's Mom?" The hostess said, "Oh, she said she was going to be out of town. I thought you knew?" My mom and I had always had a thorny relationship, but lying in order to avoid my baby shower really hurt. It may sound clichéd, but I remember how much I really just wanted my mom throughout my pregnancy. Her rejection hurt terribly; it was a major stressor.

Increased anxiety is the price we pay for our cocooning and isolation, as we distance from the communities that used to be our "herds": extended families, neighborhoods, places of worship, community service organizations, or just plain old "visiting" (how quaint and archaic that word has become!).

Americans now have dangerously few communities left in our lives, and we must stop living in denial. We must address our anxiety with the same urgency we bring to climate change or the budget deficit. If lions, elephants, or chimpanzees were to abandon the community structure of their herds, they would quickly go extinct. To imagine that the human animal is different is to live in denial.

Our social isolation increases each year, but we don't notice that our household anxiety is also slowly, imperceptibly, notching up.

We Don't Realize How Stressed We Are. We Are Living In Denial.

We may not realize we are living more stressful lives today, because stress manifests itself in many forms that a parent may not recognize. I remember working with one New York City mother whose child had increasingly serious behavior problems. When I first asked about her pregnancy, she dismissed my query as irrelevant, saying that she had an easy, stress-free pregnancy.

But over several conversations, she recalled that her family had to move out of state on very short notice during her pregnancy, and just before the move they had gone on a two-week road trip with her toddler son, her often-irritable father, and her stepmother with whom there was a lot of tension and conflict. She noted in passing that, during this car trip, she had developed a severely painful case of sciatica.

To her, the shooting pain in her hip and legs had nothing to do with her family's "getting on her nerves." She didn't see how her sciatica might be a reaction to stress, because after all, sciatica is a common ailment among pregnant women, right?

This mother only began to wonder about a mind-body connection when she found that chiropractors, acupuncture, and drugs did nothing for her hip pain. And yet, after she began seeing a physician at New York University School of Medicine who specializes in the mind-body connection, her sciatica went away almost overnight and never returned.

The prenatal stress of a sudden move and a high-drama car trip may or may not have been a factor in subsequent behavior problems of this mother's baby. But this story does show how subjective our self-perceptions of stress can be.

For example, think of all the times you have noticed someone who speaks glowingly about the chump they married, or is wildly optimistic about their career prospects when you know their personality will never get them past the first interview. Have you ever thought, "How can that person be so blind about the spouse they married? How can they fool themselves about landing that big job? They haven't got a chance!"

Humans can intuitively sense when someone is deluding themselves, and we are experts at pointing out when those around us are living in denial. But denial is extremely difficult to spot in ourselves.

Living in denial is a powerful defense mechanism in the human mind, particularly when it comes to handling stress. Most people prefer to pretend they are not upset, rather than acknowledging just how anxious they really are.

For example, most of us would readily agree that, when someone is anxious or stressed, they tend to be more irritable. Yet when we ourselves are under stress, we may not realize that we have become critical or overreactive. Instead, we tend to believe that we are being calm and reasonable, while "our spouse (or boss, or child) sure is annoying today…"

This self-delusion is important to a pregnancy because a mother-to-be may not realize how stressed she was until later, if ever. One person's self-report of stress levels may be very different from, say, an objective blood test showing the actual levels of stress hormones coursing through her veins.

In short, our society in general may not realize just how much more stressed-out we have become, or that today's stress is different from the stress our ancestors knew. But how is it different? How can stress be a major risk factor in today's epidemic of child problems, since the human race has always known stress? It must have been pretty stressful to be a Londoner in 1940, or an American in 1776. How could today's lifestyle be more stressful than ever?

The difference is *isolation*. Women in the past endured stressors like war, poverty, and illness *together*—with someone—whether husband, parents, relatives, or girl friends, in a community. In 1776, Americans put together a ragtag army of farmers and tradesmen who found strength in numbers and overcame their oppressors. In 1940, Londoners banded together and built community during the Nazi bombardments. Observers remarked on the amazing level of cooperation among thousands of families sleeping cramped together in subway stations night after night. And women took over American factories during wartime and built the tools of our victory.

Until recently, people had many levels of social support throughout their community to help them cope with stress. Today, we may not even realize how much more time we spend alone, and how many more stress hormones are floating around in our bloodstreams because of our isolation.

To summarize this chapter, our sky-high stress levels have their source in the isolation of our lives today. Humans are social animals, with a primal need for "social grooming" in the form of visiting with fellow members of our tribes, clans, and herds. The fact that we spend less time socializing these days explains a big part of the growing anxiety we feel on a daily basis.

We need to understand how our increasing isolation makes us more stressed and irritable, which causes more tension in relationships, which causes us to avoid relationships, which increases our isolation and, in turn, our stress.

Knowledge is power, and we have to realize we're caught in a vicious circle before we can begin to change. Unfortunately, we tend to live in such denial about our stress levels and isolation that it's difficult to become aware enough of this vicious circle in order to step out of it.

In Chapter 8, we will peel away a few layers of our denial, as we learn how evolution programmed our ancestors for stress as a survival mechanism—an instinct that may have outlived its usefulness.

Chapter 8

Today's Parents Have Gone Primal

A 2005 Associated Press-Ipsos poll found that nearly 70 percent of Americans said they believed that people are more rude now than they were 20 or 30 years ago, and children are especially rude. In a 2002 survey by Public Agenda, a nonpartisan and nonprofit public opinion research group, only 9 percent of adults said that children they observed in public were "respectful toward adults."

In 2004, more than one in three teachers told Public Agenda pollsters they had seriously considered leaving their profession or knew a colleague who had left because of "intolerable" student behavior. But teachers feel helpless to do anything about it. More than 80 percent of the educators polled said they had no choice but to be soft on discipline "because they can't count on parents or schools to support them."

And as Judith Warner writes in her *New York Times* column, "The pressure to do well is up. The demand to do good is down, way down, particularly if it's the kind of do-gooding that doesn't show up on a college application."

In the last chapter, I introduced the vicious circle of how our growing stress levels were increasing our irritability and antisocial behavior, which in turn increased our isolation. In this chapter, we will examine how our growing isolation, stress levels, and anti-social behavior have become a vicious circle that now impacts our children's health in ways we never foresaw. We'll look at two points:

- Our increasing stress triggers our fight-or-flight response more often; and
- Our stress response was a valuable evolutionary adaptation for our ancestors, but today it has become a hindrance to both society's and our children's well-being.

Our Increasing Stress Triggers Our Fight-or-Flight Response More Often

With more stress hormones in their system, parents spend much more time in fight-or-flight mode than before. They will fight to secure any advantage for their child, or flee from anyone who has ticked them off. In the past, people recognized the need for cooperation in communities. Neighbors made attempts at reconciliation because "this is a small town, after all."

Today, after an argument both neighbors and family members are more likely to just say, "To heck with them," and cut themselves off from each other. Unfortunately, isolation breeds stress, which triggers more fight-or-flight, which in turn breeds more tension and isolation.

Our levels of politesse, good sportsmanship, and fair play are dwindling. Most parents no longer defer to the judgment of teachers, coaches, or clergy. Internet bullying is more savage than ever. Parents don't even bother anymore to find out the truth about a playground dispute; instead, they blindly defend their child, regardless of the facts.

For example, a friend told me her six-year-old daughter was sitting on the handrail of a neighbor's deck one summer afternoon when the neighbor's son pushed her over backwards and she fell several feet. Thankfully, the girl wasn't seriously hurt, but when she complained to the boy's mother, the mother waved the girl away, saying "Boys will be boys." Amazingly, less than 24 hours later, this same mother was screaming at the little girl for not including her son in a game with other kids. The irony of the situation was completely lost on this woman, who felt no compunction about screaming at someone else's child in defense of her own. For her, there was no consideration of right or wrong. She would defend her child regardless of his behavior.

Child psychiatrist Alvin Rosenfeld explains how parenting has changed:

> *Once upon a time, parenting was largely about training children to take their proper place in their community, which, in large measure, meant learning to play by the rules and cooperate.... There was a time when there was a certain code of conduct by which you viewed the character of a person, and you needed that code of conduct to have your place in the community.*

Today's parents justify outrageous behavior with the popular mantra of, "I need to do what's best for my child," but what that really means is, "It's every man for himself." Dan Kindlon, a Harvard University child psychologist, says, "Parents who want their children to succeed more than anything teach them to value and prioritize achievement above all else— including other people."

Columnist Judith Warner described how today's parents are too focused on making sure that their kids are successful in school and on the soccer field. Parents don't seem to have noticed that the competitive traits they are cultivating in their children to assure their success are exactly the traits that are helping to break down civility in society.

As our sense of civility and community breaks down, it's hardly surprising that our sense of alienation and stress increases. Our fight-or-flight mode has become more persistent and chronic than in generations past.

The distinction between "chronic" and "acute" is an important one. As Elizabeth Verdick, whom I introduced at the beginning to Part 2, pointed out, war, illness, and loss are stressful, but only for acute, relatively short periods. Our ancestors may have felt acute stress for a while, but soon their stress levels returned to normal. Today's stress appears to be chronic, marked by a slow, imperceptible ratcheting up that never returns to previous, baseline levels. Wendy Cox, a bureau chief for a major news outlet, describes it this way: "My husband and I both have very busy professional lives: we've got three kids, aging parents, needy siblings and we're constantly walking the line between happy hubbub and utter, total, soul-destroying chaos."

Today, it's as if our families have sprung a leak, and are slowly sinking in a sea of anxiety. If many of us feel overwhelmed, it's because we are. In many unconscious ways we have already begun thrashing our limbs, as if our bodies realize we are drowning, but somehow our brains remain in denial that stress has already filled the room up to our chests, and will eventually submerge us completely. It's time to recognize our situation and do something to improve it immediately. Perhaps the best way to raise our awareness of our stress levels is by learning where stress came from in the first place. Let's take a look at the evolutionary origins of stress.

What We Call "Stress" Is Actually Anxiety—A Primal Survival Instinct

We tend to think of stress as an unpleasant feeling of anxiety we experience when life gets difficult. We tend to believe that, if we removed those external stressors, then that unpleasant feeling would go away.

Not so. Anxiety is more than just an unpleasant feeling. It is a primal instinct, which evolved in us because it was key to our survival. Anxiety helps animals to anticipate possible danger and triggers our fight-or-flight response.

In our caveman days, predators or enemies were "stressors," and anxiety helped us to scan our environment for danger, always trying to foresee potential threats before they happened.

A useful metaphor is to think of anxiety as a nervous soldier on guard duty, ever-vigilant and ready to protect us from danger by mobilizing our fight-or-flight response. A calm guard might focus objectively on the real movements and noises in the bushes. However, a "nervous soldier" might jump at a shadow, or the slightest rustling noise in the bush. That nervous soldier may be filled with all kinds of insecurities and stories he has heard that make him tense. This greatly increases the likelihood that he will overreact and trip the alarm even when it's not necessary. The nervous soldier can be trigger-happy.

Back when humans lived in the wilderness, it was okay to have a trigger-happy brain and jump to conclusions. An anxious, quick-and-dirty appraisal was all we needed to act. If, for example, we overreacted and fled from a perceived threat that turned out to be nothing, no harm done—we just got some extra exercise that day. Anxiety empowered our ancestors to protect their families from danger, so they could safely raise offspring. This stress-response served us well for the last 50,000 generations, and through survival of the fittest, our ancestors passed on this genetic advantage.

Remember our Chapter 5 discussion of the predictive adaptive response? Now you know where it fits in, from an evolutionary perspective. Basically, the predictive adaptive response is trying to create an appropriately-nervous "soldier on guard duty" to protect the fetus once it is born into its mother's environment.

The problem is, civilization has evolved much more quickly than our brains have, and likewise for our predictive adaptive responses. Daily life is now much safer, as the rule of law protects more families and property than, say, in the Middle Ages. Improved nutrition has greatly decreased the odds we might die young. We now live 60 percent longer than we did only 100 years ago.

Dr. Marc Siegel of NYU School of Medicine writes in the Washington Post about how, despite the relative safety of modern society, we humans still behave as if it's a jungle out there. We're overreacting to everything lately, so it's no surprise that we're overreacting to our spouses more, and getting divorced more:

> *Of course we can't just turn off fear; it's part of our psychological makeup from birth, integral to the elaborate system of self-protection that has preserved the human species for millenniums. But lately, you could*

*argue, the fear component of that system has been malfunctioning…
It used to be that a person could die from a scratch. Now we take
effective antibiotics at the first sign of trouble. Public health measures
dictate standards for drinkable water and breathable air. Our garbage
is removed quickly. We live temperature-controlled, largely disease-
controlled lives.*

*And yet, we worry more than ever before. The natural dangers are no
longer there, but the response mechanisms are turned on much of the time.
We implode, turning our adaptive fear mechanism into a maladaptive
panicked response.*

What Dr. Siegel calls "our adaptive fear mechanism" is another way
of describing the flight response in fight-or-flight. And anxiety is our primal,
instinctive trigger of fight-or-flight. So anxiety used to be a valuable survival
instinct in our caveman days, but when our brain's stress response kicks in,
one of the first things it does is to hijack the part of the brain responsible
for reasonable, thoughtful responses. So, our brain panics and makes snap
judgments based on scanty evidence, in the name of speed.

Back when we lived in the wilderness, to err on the side of fight-or-
flight was fine. But today our anxious overreactions may cause us to criticize,
fight, or flee from our loved ones. Today's interactions are much more
complex than eat-or-be-eaten. We can't walk into the company boardroom
with a caveman's club, or sit at our family dinner table, poised to pounce or
flee. Negotiating all the gray areas of modern relationships requires much
more subtlety and nuance than our ancient anxiety instinct offers. We're
trying to conduct our daily life with outdated equipment inside our heads.

In other words, it's hard for us to respond thoughtfully when our
anxiety is running the show. From road rage, divorce, or helicopter parenting
to depression, insomnia, and excessive medication use, we're stuck in chronic
overreaction mode.

Of course, we might not call it "chronic overreaction mode." We
might call this overreactive state having "a chip on your shoulder." The

problem is, an overreactive state is easier to see in someone else than in ourselves. We humans tend to believe our thoughts are rational most of the time, so we believe our judgments and criticisms are objective. The truth, however, is we're mostly reacting to irrational feelings based on the snap judgment of our anxiety run amok. Our buttons get pushed, we anxiously overreact to a perceived slight, and then things escalate. We don't see the role we play in creating the drama in our lives.

To sum up this chapter, our increasing stress triggers our fight-or-flight response more often in our day-to-day lives, which leads to more antisocial behavior and more isolation. Anxiety began as a survival mechanism in our ancestors, but has spiraled out of control in modern society and impacts our children's health in ways we never foresaw. Generally speaking, increased parental stress has triggered a heightened predictive adaptive response *in utero*, which is unfortunately programming the fetal brain with an overreactive stress-response system.

Living in today's Age of Anxiety has left us in chronic fight-or-flight mode, and our reactions to threats are not always guided by our thoughtful intellect. Anxiety has overrun our thin veneer of civilized politesse, and we've gone primal, overreacting to the smallest slight as if we were under attack: from road rage to assault on the sidelines of a children's soccer game. And couples increasingly fight-or-flee from their marriages. In the next chapter, we'll examine why more marriages today are more troubled, and why they are affecting our children much more than we thought.

Chapter 9

Your Marriage May Be Much More Stressful Than You Think

Throughout this book you've heard me say that relationships (or the lack thereof) are our main source of stress, and now I'll explain why. As Dr. Marc Siegel describes above, humans have evolved a stress response that does not match our modern levels of danger, so we overreact to everything. This leaves us chronically in fight-or-flight mode, which makes all our relationships, especially spousal and family relationships, much more tense.

So, we tend to fight for a while, then "flee" each other. Of course we never think of our flight-response as such. We might call it, "avoiding that jerk," or "life is too short," but most likely, we don't call it anything at all. We never consciously decide to avoid our spouse, or that relative with whom we used to be close. Instead, we allow other people and activities to take precedence. It's only when we look up, six months or a year later, that we realize we're not as close with our spouse or that relative as we used to be. Our flight-response is instinctive, unconscious, and stealthy.

Speaking of stealth, we haven't even noticed that our increasing isolation from our loved ones and our communities has been slowly, stealthily ratcheting up our anxiety. We are no longer scratching the itch—that primal need for reassurance that we find in bonding and social grooming. But our isolation and the resulting anxiety have now hit critical mass and created a vicious circle. As our anxiety increases, so does our irritability, which causes more tension in our relationships and triggers our fight-or-flight response more often. When our spouse or relative reacts to our fight-or-flight response, it further escalates the tension, which in turn makes us even more likely to flee this uncomfortable relationship and isolate ourselves. Again: we never call it a flight response or isolation. We call it "I'm busy," or "I'm swamped with work lately…" or "Just give me a sec to check my messages here…"

In the last chapter, we looked at how today's parents have gone primal: over-stressed, overreactive, constantly in competition over even the smallest of issues, and perpetually in fight-or-flight mode. If you walk away from this book with only one insight, I hope you will begin to see how so much of our behavior is governed by our anxiety, which triggers our primal, unconscious fight-or-flight response, and it plays particular havoc on our most intimate of relationships, our marriages—although we may not have noticed.

This chapter will help us become aware of how our marriages are vulnerable to stress, and how that impacts both the parents' and the children's well-being. In this chapter, we will examine several issues:

1) The real reason today's marriages are more troubled;
2) Our fight-or-flight response governs more of our behavior than we realize;
3) The hidden cost of bottling-up our marital discord;
4) The Myth: Parents' arguing traumatizes their kids;
5) Today we have higher expectations of marriage, therefore, more stress.

The Real Reason Today's Marriages Are More Troubled

Here's the real reason modern marriages tend to go bad more often than in the past: if a scientist places two rats on a metal grid and then passes an electric current through the grid, every time the rats feel an electric shock they will attack each other. Likewise with humans: when life gets stressful, we instinctively pick a fight with our spouse.

Let's return to those shocked rats. They fight because their stress response has kicked into fight-or-flight mode, and so they'll attack whoever is closest to them. It's not logical. It's instinctive, it's primal, and it's called scapegoating.

Scapegoating is a primal instinct that humans share with other animals. Any lab researcher can tell you the remarkable similarity the rat brain structure has to human brain structure. The similarity only seems shocking because humans have largely forgotten that we are animals, and we share with animals a little-known, unconscious instinct to scapegoat those around us. This is what drives couples apart. But a simple awareness of our scapegoating instinct can transform how we view our marriages.

Scapegoating is an ancient defense mechanism in the brain that allows us to off-load our anxious reactivity onto others. Best-selling author and primatologist Frans de Waal describes our tendency to blame others as one of our least conscious, yet most powerful instincts. This displacement of blame happens so often, in so many animal species, that it must be hardwired into us, dating back eons.

From a survival-of-the-fittest perspective, scapegoating was a valuable adaptation. Back in our caveman days, a little bit of anxious reactivity was a useful survival instinct, because it triggered our fight-or-flight response and kept us on our toes.

But if too much anxiety overwhelmed our brains we might shut down—unable to hunt, gather, or procreate. So scapegoating probably evolved to help us lighten our load of anxiety by off-loading it onto those around us, which cleared our minds to better focus on competing for scarce resources. The Blame Game is a primitive survival instinct.

Of course, blaming others for our suffering is nothing new. The term "scapegoat" comes from Hebrew and describes an ancient Jewish ritual of atonement during Yom Kippur. People believed God made them suffer as punishment for their sins.

So their atonement ritual involved two goats. One was sacrificed as a symbolic "payment" to God for the debt they had amassed by their sinning.

The other (the "escape goat") was driven into the wilderness, symbolically carrying the sins of the people on his back. This was how people paid for their sins in order to free themselves from their suffering. That's why today a scapegoat usually refers to an innocent person who is blamed for the suffering or wrongdoing of others.

Here's the key lesson: When we criticize our spouses, we tend to believe we are pointing out true, objective faults. But in fact, blaming our spouse may just be our anxiety talking. As discussed above, people with higher anxiety are more likely to overreact, so spouses with high anxiety have a greater tendency to fight-or-flee with or from each other, which may lead to a downward spiral that sours their marriage. When the going gets tough, rats, humans, and many other species tend to scapegoat.

This is actually great news, because now that we understand this, we can give up searching for a Spouse-Upgrade. Our marriages will fare better when we let go of the illusion that the grass would be greener with a different mate.

If people wore their thoughts on their sleeve, most of our sleeves would say, "My life is my spouse's fault." When we find ourselves dissatisfied with our lives, we rarely spend time doing the painful, confronting work of examining our own role in our discontent. Instead, we look at the people in our lives with dismay. At best, we might say, "Gee, I was a dummy to pick *him* for a spouse." But more often, we'll think, "I had no idea he was going to be like this when I married him."

Paradoxically, as we become more self-aware of our own shortcomings, it makes it easier to accept those of our spouse. When we realize what a piece of work we are ourselves, suddenly we can look at our spouse with more humility, and perhaps even gratitude that they stuck with us all these years. My wife and I find tremendous freedom in acknowledging that one of us is no better than the other—we simply have different faults.

Sure, we all know folks who would swear their ex-spouse was a dud and the chemistry they felt at first was dead wrong. But they may be kidding themselves. Their second spouse may have different traits, but the basic ways humans cope with anxiety—fight, flight, or scapegoating—are always beneath the surface. Until we become aware of our own anxiety and scapegoating instinct, we simply drag all of our baggage into our next marriage as well. That's why the divorce rate for second marriages is 60 percent, and for third marriages it's 73 percent. Things may *seem* different in a new relationship, especially at first, but the human mind is a powerful thing. Perhaps we want so badly to believe that our first spouse was a dud that we work extra-hard to make our next marriage succeed. That way, we can "prove" that the problem lay with our former spouse, and there's nothing wrong with us.

Our Fight-Or-Flight Response Governs More of Our Behavior Than We Realize

As our anxiety increases, different people exhibit different behaviors. Some people become more irritable and scapegoat those around them more. But others rely more on a *flight response* that increases with stress: we call it "keeping the peace in a marriage," but it's a flight-response all the same.

Our increased anxiety triggers our brain's stress response more often, so we spend more time in fight-or-flight mode than ever before. But almost none of us realize that our flight response is the real silent killer of relationships. Our increasing tendency to walk away from tension in relationships is actually our flight response gone awry, and it causes the slow, hidden erosion of marriages and community.

The heightened stress levels of today's parents leave them more irritable and overreactive, but couples may deny this, saying, "We seldom argue." However, research suggests marital problems are a major stressor for couples, but not for the reason we might assume. Most couples believe that if they don't fight much, then they don't have relationship problems. But our silent flight response is a huge relationship problem and a big source of stress in today's families, because we don't even realize that "flight" is just as harmful as "fight."

Many couples worry that arguing leads to divorce. Sure, when our fight-response is triggered and we argue, it feels unpleasant, so we think it's noble when we "keep the peace" in our marriage. But "keeping the peace" may be our *flight* response in disguise. This is the real silent killer in marriage, and we're not even aware of it.

The Hidden Cost of Bottling Up Our Marital Discord

It should be obvious that blaming the mother for a child's disorder is both fruitless and wrong. Rather, today's parents need to realize that marital problems and the flight-response, that silent killer of marriages, are a leading contributor to stress hormone levels in mothers, which has unintended consequences for both the mother's and the child's health. A good marriage cannot cure all stress, but a good marriage certainly contributes to a calmer, happier life.

A *New York Times* article describes a link between wives who avoid conflict, and the health consequences:

> *The tendency to bottle up feelings during a fight is known as self-silencing. For men, it may simply be a calculated but harmless decision to keep the peace. But when women stay quiet, it takes a surprising physical toll.*

> *"When you're suppressing communication and feelings during conflict with your husband, it's doing something very negative to your physiology, and in the long term it will affect your health," said Elaine Eaker, an epidemiologist in Gaithersburg, Md., who was the study's lead author. "This doesn't mean women should start throwing plates at their husbands, but there needs to be a safe environment where both spouses can equally communicate."*

> *Other studies led by Dana Crowley Jack, a professor of interdisciplinary studies at Western Washington University in Bellingham, Wash., have linked the self-silencing trait to numerous psychological and physical health risks, including depression, eating disorders and heart disease.*

Bottling up marital discord harms not only the mother but also the child. In a study by researchers at the University of Notre Dame, 22 children watched 12 brief videos showing the kind of non-verbal conflict between couples that one might observe in a typical family. The children reacted just as viscerally to non-verbal tension or conflict as to overt arguments. In other words, kids notice everything, whether verbal or nonverbal. And children interpret conflict between their parents as a threat to their security, which elicits a strong negative emotional response in them.

The researchers concluded that children interpret a fight-or-flight-response—even if it's non-verbal, such as passive-aggressive actions or The Silent Treatment—to be just as threatening to their security as a verbal fight-response.

At the Woman and Children's Hospital of Buffalo, Dr. Bea Wood analyzed the families of 272 children with asthma to see if a negative emotional climate might be a trigger for asthma symptoms. A negative emotional climate was associated with symptoms of depression in the children, which increased their likelihood of having asthma symptoms. In this and other studies, Dr. Wood underlines the importance of intervening in the family's relationship processes when treating depressed children with asthma.

At Marquette University's Department of Psychology, Dr. Astrida Kaugar's review of psychological research on asthma onset suggests that family emotional characteristics, including spousal conflict, are a key influence for the onset of pediatric asthma.

Couples can fool themselves that by avoiding arguments in front of the kids they dodge a bullet. But they can't fool their kids. It's *not* arguing in front of the kids that causes the greatest harm. It's the silent, free-floating, unresolved tension that kids absorb and turn into acting-out and symptoms.

Next, we will examine whether arguing in front of the kids really causes the harm we have assumed.

Myth: Parents' Arguing Traumatizes the Kids

My grandmother once told me of an argument her parents were having, when grandma was only about 10. "Please stop fighting!" my brave grandmother requested. "We'll stop fighting as soon as you stop fighting with your siblings!" was the spirited reply. "That shut me up," my grandmother laughed….

An article at a parenting website debunks one of modern parenting's biggest myths—that arguing traumatizes our children. Mark Cummings of Notre Dame and his colleague Patrick Davies recently published the book Marital Conflict and Children, which suggests that parents have overestimated the harm arguing does to their children. They write:

Children are very aware of non-verbal anger. Overt anger is not always good either, but if you're angry but not saying anything, the only people being fooled by that are the parents. Kids don't care about blow-ups—the style of fighting doesn't matter, whether it's the slow burn, or if you're really angry or really loud. If parents work it out, the kids don't care. They care about the meaning of the conflict.

We did a longitudinal study on how kids interpret it...If parents get really loud it might be temporarily distressing to the child, but there is no long-term feeling about it. But you can't pretend you're working it out. Kids are not fooled if you're pretending to get along.

[W]e've now found that it's not fighting that's destructive, but how parents handle the fight. Conflict is unavoidable—in most marriages it can be a frequent, everyday occurrence. Our key finding is that if parents handle the conflict well, meaning constructively, it's not the anger that bothers kids, it's when the anger threatens to negatively affect the family. In fact, if [parents] do work it out, many times kids come away with a positive emotion.

Cummings' research suggests that, instead of suppressing conflict and pretending it's not there, parents need to learn how to deal with conflict on a daily basis, and model conflict resolution for the benefit of their children's future relationships. (My two favorite books on conflict are written by a psychiatrist and a Buddhist priest.)

So yes, we need to deal better with tension in our marriages, but it's also helpful to understand why there is more tension in today's marriages than in the past. Beneath our awareness, our expectations of what a marriage should be are much higher than in the past. A quick look at the history of marriage may offer some insight as to how our frustrated expectations are increasing our stress levels in marriage.

Today We Have Higher Expectations of Marriage, Therefore More Stress

Historically, in many cultures marriage was a business transaction where couples had few romantic expectations. Parents would negotiate with other parents to improve the financial or social standing of both families through the marriage of their children. Women were property, and a dowry sweetened the deal.

The concept of love was nowhere to be found in this calculus of money, power, and status. Couples often found themselves naked on the night of their honeymoon with spouses they had only met that day.

Even in the relatively recent history of Western cultures like America, where marrying for love was the tradition, divorce was not an option, because the feelings of one individual were only a tiny factor in a marriage. Marriage was a contract uniting the finances, power, and reputation of two families. To dissolve such a union had ramifications for one's entire clan, so this was no small matter to be left to the capricious feelings of the newlyweds. A woman who chose divorce disgraced herself and her family, and ran a great risk of becoming homeless and destitute.

In other words, failure was not an option.

Both spouses therefore had to grin and bear it, making the best of the marriage they had been pushed into. Spouses strove for some kind of peaceful, tolerable living arrangement, and hoped it might grow into a companionship to sustain them through raising a family and growing old together. They had no choice but to use diplomacy and deference with their in-laws, and they relied heavily on the outside community for their social needs. Men spent their time with other men, whether in the ancient context of hunting parties or the more recent ones of business or athletic clubs, service organizations, or the local pub. Women spent their time with other women, grinding corn, preparing food together, participating in quilting circles, attending religious activities, or joining civic organizations.

Although the concept may sound strange to us today, in the past, whether one had a good marriage or not didn't matter as much. Each spouse spent so much time with their relatives, friends, and community organizations that they didn't have to turn to their spouse for their social needs. One could find fulfillment in life without relying on one's spouse for social support.

Don't get me wrong. I am in no way advocating a return to some romanticized version of the Middle Ages. Life then was, for nearly everyone, nasty, brutish, and short. Women had few choices or options. Arranged marriages perpetuated an unequal and oppressive social order. But it is crucial to the future of our families that we become aware of how today's marriage is very different.

Today, the stakes are much higher for a marriage, as the marital relationship has become the sole source of social support for many spouses. Our lives are much more transient, and we no longer live in the same house or neighborhood as our parents, grandparents, uncles, aunts, and cousins. We leave behind the other members of our village in the name of career or financial betterment. While many improvements can come from these new freedoms, they have also had a huge and unanticipated impact on our families.

We now expect much more from our spouse and our marriage than we ever did before. Our modern, transient lifestyles have taken us away from our traditional support networks, leaving us increasingly dependent on our spouses for our social and emotional needs. Marriage was once seen as just one small strand in the complex social web of relationships within families, clans, and communities. Now, increasingly, marriage has become the only boat into which we load our expectations of love and fulfillment, as well as all our social and emotional needs.

And that boat sinks more often than in the past.

Our social support networks have been dwindling over the decades, and the concept of the Love Marriage has been growing for centuries. Troubadours of the Middle Ages sang and wrote poems about true love's beauty, and dreams of love have increasingly filled our consciousness and our literature over the centuries.

But now marriage is caught in the stormy seas of social change, where two powerful currents have muddied the waters:

1) The rise of the Love Marriage, and

2) The decline of our social support networks.

The timing of these two currents could not have been more important: Marriage has been a contract between families for millennia, but suddenly that tradition fades from view, and love becomes the ultimate motivation for marriage. At the same time, the decline of our social support networks suddenly puts tremendous pressure on our marriages as our main source of social and emotional fulfillment.

Equal rights for women granted them an unprecedented level of financial and social independence, so for the first time, women were free to enter or exit a marriage when they pleased. For the first time ever, couples, and especially women, could ask a question they never dared consider before:

"Do I feel fulfilled in my marriage?"

At first glance, this seems like an excellent question, indicative of wonderful new levels of freedom and choice. Today, women can choose to divorce without facing financial ruin, homelessness, or permanent social stigma. This has been tremendously empowering for women in problem marriages and a critical jump forward toward equal rights. But as the dissolution of marriages has become more acceptable, we also must face some of the side-effects that come as a consequence. One of those side-effects may be that the pendulum has swung from the oppressive marriages of yesteryear to an idealized, unattainable ideal of marriage today.

The rise of the Love Marriage has left us expecting and demanding nothing less than a happy, fulfilling emotional connection and communication that will last for decades with our spouse. A recent survey found that 94 percent of twenty-somethings seek a soul-mate more than any other trait in a spouse. "Seeking a compatible mate who shares similar values is not new, but what is new and surprising is that the soul-mate ideal has become the most desired marital partner characteristic for this age group—surpassing religion, economics and even the ability to be a good mother or father," states David Popenoe of the National Marriage Project.

The pressure to find our soul-mate has recently doubled, because the decline of our social support networks has left us not only demanding but actually *needing* a Love Marriage. Finding our soul-mate now seems to be our only remaining option for fulfillment in this transient society, because we have grown to depend on our marriages for most of our social and emotional needs. Lastly, the rise of women's marital and financial freedom has given spouses the option of just walking away if they do not feel their social and emotional needs are being met. We now have the option of trying again, with a different spouse, to see if perhaps the grass will be greener next time. Or the time after that.

This is the side-effect of freedom: the freedom to leave a marriage, sometimes too soon. We may have forgotten the power of keeping our word. The vow to stay with someone for richer or poorer, in sickness and in health, is a powerful thing. Taking one's vow seriously is a great motivator for finding a way to make things work. Sure, one could say they're "stuck with their spouse for life," or that person could also say, "We refused to give up, so we found ways to make it work, and we're better for it."

My point is that we may not realize we are still in the middle of a social revolution. And like many revolutions, the pendulum may have swung too far from one extreme to the other. We have gone from one extreme of loveless, oppressive marriages to the other extreme of holding such sky-high expectations for the perfect Love Marriage that maintaining any marriage becomes next to impossible. The longer we remain in this extreme, the more painful divorces we experience. Not only do we suffer as adults, we unwittingly pass that weight and anxiety on to our children.

It is important to recognize just how far the pendulum has swung, in order to get it back to a healthy middle ground. Until we lower our expectations of fulfillment in modern marriage, we are doomed to be unfulfilled. As long as we ask, "Am I fulfilled in my marriage?" we may be doomed to divorce because no marriage can survive the sky-high level of expectations inherent in that question.

To summarize this chapter, scapegoating plays a large role in modern marriage as our fight-or-flight response causes us to blame our spouse for our problems. Our flight-response, and bottling up our marital discord, can also be highly destructive. Our high expectations of marriage to fulfill our every social need can really set us up for disappointment.

In the next chapter, we will examine a way many couples use to deal with that disappointment. Rather than filing papers in court, many of today's couples simply ignore the tension in their marriages, and throw themselves into parenting—the ultimate flight-response.

Chapter 10

Your Marriage Affects Your Child More Than You Think

Madeline Levine is a child psychologist and author. In her book, *The Price of Privilege*, she confirms that kids are definitely attuned not only to the emotional pipeline between them and each parent, but also to the emotional pipeline *between* their parents:

> *Children can read the needs of their parents remarkably well. They know that the mother who spends a disproportionate amount of time and energy inserting herself into her child's life is likely to be fending off her own unhappiness. She needs to be overinvolved, and, in an unfortunately common psychological drama, her child is willing to sacrifice his own needs to meet hers. Parental over-involvement and intrusion are typically indications that a parent's own needs are not being adequately met. When a marriage is cold, a child's bed is a warm place to be. (Page 140)*

In this chapter, we will examine two points:

- The trend of "emotional divorce" in today's marriages, where couples become so emotionally distant that one spouse ends up more married to their child than to his or her spouse;

- The relief of acknowledging our sky-high stress levels, and stepping out of the vicious circle that created them.

Parents Who Marry Their Children Instead of Their Spouse

It's no accident that intrusive parenting is a growing trend. Intrusive parenting may be filling a void in the marriages of today, which some experts refer to as the "emotional divorce."

In an emotional divorce, the husband maintains the requisite small-talk and routines of marriage, but he has essentially checked out of the relationship, and the couple live almost like roommates. This behavior appears peaceful, but it is merely a primal flight response in disguise, and it produces great anxiety in the household.

We're kidding ourselves that all is well as we "flee" our spouses every day. We turn to our electronic screens, work long hours, shuttle our kids, co-sleep with our kids, or make up excellent reasons why we never have sex anymore.

Putting our kids first may now be our favorite way to "flee" our spouses. Parents have long known that neglect could scar a child for life, but we have gone to the other extreme, and became best friends with our child at the expense of our marriages and our children's mental health. Today's favorite way to avoid our spouses may be to throw ourselves into over-parenting.

It may seem child-friendly to marry our kids instead of our partners, but when a marriage grows distant, the household stress level soars, and then the children suffer and act out.

Since a child is so attuned to his or her parents, the parents' avoidance behaviors are a clear sign of high stress to a child (at least on an unconscious level), and that stress has a detrimental impact on their child's behavior. "There is definitely a link between high stress households and child mental health problems," says Dr. Ilana Slaff, a psychiatrist in New York who treats autistic children. "And often, mental health problems will be expressed as a physical ailment."

To compare the impact on children's mental health and behavior to two parental behaviors—arguing and withdrawing from each other—researchers at the University of Rochester studied 210 families over a three-year period. Each year, the parents were asked to discuss difficult topics in their marriage while being videotaped. Experts then used well-known criteria to "code" each verbal and non-verbal cue in the videotapes on a scale of "bonding vs. emotional withdrawal" behaviors. Meanwhile, the children's behaviors were determined from interviews with parents and teachers, and from the child's academic records.

These data allowed researchers to compare ups or downs in children's behavior to how bonded or withdrawn their parents were at that same time period. They concluded that interparental hostility and withdrawal or emotional unavailability had a direct impact on children's internalizing behaviors (such as depression or illness) and externalizing behaviors (such as non-compliance or acting out). In other words, the more parents were in fight-or-flight mode, the more their children acted-out or developed symptoms of illness.

Today's parents tend to marry their children instead of their spouse. Parents believe this approach is child-friendly, but research shows a child-centered family is lose-lose for both the child and the parents in the long run, because it tends to produce children who are aggressive, hyperactive, depressed or socially withdrawn. A 2009 *New York Times* article describes the phenomenon:

> "*In the last 20 years, everyone's been talking about how important it is for fathers to be involved [in child-rearing],*" said Sara S. McLanahan, a professor of Sociology and Public Affairs at Princeton. "*But now the idea is that the better the couple gets along, the better it is for the child.*"

Her research, part of a project based at Princeton and called the Fragile Families and Child Wellbeing Study, found that when couples scored high on positive relationship traits like willingness to compromise, expressing affection or love for their partner, encouraging or helping partners to do things that were important to them, and having an absence of insults and criticism, the father was significantly more likely to be engaged with his children.

Dr. McLanahan's research shows that a family where the marriage takes priority is win-win for both parents and children. Like the flight attendant's safety instructions for parents to put on their own oxygen masks before attending to their children, focusing on a quality marital relationship reduces stress and tension in the household. The *New York Times* goes on to describe McLanahan's findings:

> *[A focus on improving the marriage produced fathers who] became more emotionally involved with their children, and the children were much less aggressive, hyperactive, depressed or socially withdrawn than children of fathers in the control group...*

> *[Couples that focused on improving their marriage had] less parental stress and more marital happiness than the other parents studied, suggesting that the critical difference was not greater involvement by the fathers in child-rearing but greater emotional support between couples.*

McLanahan's research challenges the widely-held assumption that increased paternal involvement increases children's well-being. In fact, a happier marriage improved children's well-being; the increased paternal involvement in child-rearing only *appeared* to be the cause. Parents jumped to the wrong conclusion.

That said, it may feel strange at first to let go of the belief that the more attention we give our kids, the better they'll turn out. To focus more attention on our marriages seems counter-cultural. But while many parents feel sorely tempted to focus on their children, we need to re-train our brains so we understand that the best thing for both parents and children in the long run is to give regular maintenance to the marriage:

> *"Parents work all day, and feel as if they need to give every other minute to the kids," Dr. Cowan [a psychology professor at UC Berkeley] said,*

"but if they don't take care of the relationship between them, they're not taking care of the whole story."

The quality of the marriage usually determines how much time the father spends with his wife, or with his child. If the marriage is going well, the father is likely to be available more, both physically and emotionally. If the marriage is troubled, he is more likely to withdraw, either emotionally or even physically, from the marriage. And this has a greater effect on the child then we think.

At UCLA, Dr. Darby Saxbe and her colleagues surveyed the marriages of the parents of 50 fourth-grade girls. Two years later, the researchers compared marriage quality with when the daughters hit puberty. They found that when fathers had described marital dissatisfaction and mothers felt a lack of emotional support, their daughters tended to reach puberty earlier. Fathers' emotional withdrawal from the marriage was the single biggest predictor of the timing of their daughters' pubertal development.

The results of this study are consistent with evolutionary models. In the case of animals with an absent father (such as prairie dogs), the shortage of available mates means females would be better off maturing sooner, so they can mate sooner. Amazingly, this is also true in humans: human fathers who are emotionally withdrawn (even if they remain physically present) have a strong enough influence to trigger this earlier-maturing response in their daughters. Thus, the distancing behavior (flight response) of the father has the biggest impact on his daughter, and may directly affect her reproductive cycle.

It may surprise you that the state of a marriage could actually have a physiological impact on a daughter's reproductive system. But Dr. Saxbe's research is one of many studies confirming the impact an emotional divorce has on our children. It's time to look at whether we are living an emotional divorce in our marriages, even to a small degree. If we acknowledge and address the stress created by emotional divorce, we can reduce that stress and pass less baggage onto our children.

Chapter 11

Myth: The More Attention We Give Our Kids, the Better They Turn Out

Elizabeth Verdick, a mother from Saint Paul, Minn., describes today's parents as the "Supposed-To" Generation:

> *Many of us are living 'supposed-to' kinds of lives as we raise our children. We're supposed to be there for them all the time, get them into the best schools, arrange their social lives, take them to all their activities, and provide beautiful, loving homes. Magazines and TV shows portray this image for us, and it's easy to fall into a trap of trying to do everything close to perfectly. All while managing a successful career! With little social support....*

Although we parents are doing what we are allegedly Supposed To, we're not getting the results we're Supposed To get, in terms of our children's health and well-being.

This chapter will examine the following:

1) Good parenting is not about giving kids more attention;

2) It's about the "vibe" we give off; you can't fake being "casual" to your kids when you're not;

3) Children learn cooperation when treated as co-workers, not leaders of the family.

We parents are dying to "get it right" when it comes to our kids and, as previously discussed, we simultaneously expect perfectly fulfilling marriages. As a result, our expectations put enormous pressure on our marriages, and our kids pick up on the anxiety created by our sky-high expectations. Everything is so significant. Everything matters so much. If we could simply turn down the intensity of our interactions with our kids, everyone would benefit.

We have unknowingly taken Freud too far, and turned him into a caricature. The popular perception of Freud's message is that any discontent we feel as adults is because of the upsets or traumas we suffered as children. We parents therefore break our backs to provide the perfect, trauma-free childhood for our kids, full of love and affirmation, so they can grow up to be happy, successful, well-adjusted, fulfilled adults. But there is growing evidence that we are deluding ourselves.

In her book, *Perfect Madness: Mothering in the Age of Anxiety*, Judith Warner quotes a Washington mother who'd left a prestigious government job working on child-care policy because it allowed her no time with her kids:

> *The children are the center of the household and everything goes around them. You want to do everything and be everything for them because this is your job now. You take all the energy and enthusiasm you had in your career and you feel the need to be as successful raising your children as you were in the workplace. And you can make your kids totally crazy in the process. (Page 6)*

This Washington mother is a perfect example of how parents' growing isolation has left them over-stressed, fueling their tendency toward helicopter parenting and a life centered around their children. Yet although few parents have heard the term, "Vulnerable Child Syndrome," many parents can sense that, even with the best of intentions, they are making their kids crazy.

Indeed, for all our efforts, today's kids seem even more troubled and demanding, which creates even more anxious, hovering, Helicopter Parents. It's time to admit we're not getting the results we expected with our Supposed-To strategy. So, what should we change?

What Good Parenting is REALLY About

There is one insight that would greatly improve both our marriages and our parenting if we became aware of it. Good parenting is not about giving your kids more attention.

Did you know studies show that today's parents actually spend more time with their young children than in the 1960's? If parenting is all about time and attention, why do today's children seem so much more troubled than before?

The cardinal rule of parenting should not be "The more attention you give your kids, the better they'll turn out." The cardinal rule should be, "Kids pick up on everything." More time and attention to our child doesn't have much benefit if it is fraught with guilt about neglect because we work full-time, or worry about how our child is progressing (compared to what the parenting books say), or are wracked with anxiety about keeping all the balls in the air, or beset by self-doubt about whether we are doing all we can to give our child the perfect launch. To quote Judith Warner again:

> [Today's] women were afraid of being called neurotic. So they put a little lipstick on and kept busy. They started doing their children's homework for them. They pushed their children into meaningless activities, whipped up competition within their communities—battled among friends—for the best birthday party, the best barbecue. They let their kids' social lives take over theirs, let their kids' lives consume them altogether, to give themselves, in the psychological parlance of the day, a 'sense of significance.' There was a sense, among many psychologists, that the pressures on women were cracking them apart. Tranquilizer use was on the rise; one such pill, Pacatal, was advertised as a way to "release the housewife from the grip of neurosis." (Page 38)

It's About the "Vibe" We Give Off

In short, it's not about what we do with our child, or what we say. It's more about the "vibe" we give off, because kids pick up on everything. And today our vibe might be more anxious than we realize. If kids really do notice everything, would we want them to pick up on the stuff going on in our minds most of the time?

As parents, it's time for us to acknowledge the huge, pink elephant stuffed into the room between us and our child. That elephant is our anxiety:

- The worry we have about how our child is doing;
- The self-doubt we feel about how *we* are doing as parents;
- The fear we harbor that even the smallest trauma may scar our child for life;
- The almost manic intensity we bring to parenting; and
- This anxious, hand-wringing intensity that has spawned what we now call Helicopter Parenting.

We need to realize that our personal fulfillment and our healthy relationships are the best gifts we can give our children, rather than more face time, more educational toys, more exotic vacations, more tennis instruction, or other resume-building activities. Best of all, our children could learn more independence—to entertain themselves and to seek their own happiness instead of waiting for us to spoon-feed it to them.

If I could wave my magic wand and reduce the stress of today's parents, I would give them a glass of wine, a friend, and an Italian village square to go socialize in every evening. We can't fake casual to our kids. We can't pretend our minds are empty, playful, and light-hearted when they are not. The only way we can reduce all the chatter in our heads that our kids are picking up on is to go socialize and have some fun ourselves. Fun, playfulness, and humor are contagious. It's hard to introduce playfulness into a room that's filled with anxious intensity, but once you've filled a room with playfulness, it's hard to introduce anxiety. We will soon learn how in Part 3.

Child-Centered Families and Dual Careers

Just as parenting began to demand much more time and attention, most households became dual-career. The scheduling demands alone were daunting, but add to that the fear parents often feel that they may be messing up their children by paying child-care centers or nannies to raise them. But when parents come home from work, they are too tired and stressed-out to take on the arduous tasks of teaching their children good manners and cooperative behavior.

Instead, parents tend to marry their children rather than their spouses, relating to their children in a personally needy way. They want to be a friend instead of a disciplinarian, and they want the precious little time they have with their children to be fabulous, so they hesitate to set healthy boundaries.

"We use kids like Prozac," says Harvard University child psychologist Dan Kindlon. "People don't necessarily feel great about their spouse or their job but the kids are the bright spot in their day. They don't want to muck up that one moment by getting yelled at [by their kids]. They don't want to hurt. They don't want to feel bad. They want to get satisfaction from their kids. They're so precious to us—maybe more than to any generation previously. What gets thrown out the window is limits. It's a lot easier to pick their towel up off the floor than to get them away from the PlayStation to do it."

Anxious chaos in the household may be the result, which is lose-lose for both child and parent. To see just how crazy we are making ourselves, let's take a look at how things used to be for families.

Parenting Then and Now: We Forgot a Couple Key Points

The image of the 1950's housewife leading a life of leisure was a tiny blip on the screen of history, if it ever existed at all. Women have always worked long, hard hours, just like men. Our ancestors were hunters, gatherers, and farmers, toiling from dawn to dusk to provide for their families.

In the past, a child was not the de-facto president of the family, with veto power over the family's meals *("I don't eat chicken!")* and activities. Children were co-workers. When they were infants, their mothers slung them on their back as they went to work. As toddlers, kids would play nearby as their mothers toiled in the fields. Once they were old enough, children worked side-by-side with their parents, hunting, farming, cleaning, canning, or caring for younger siblings.

In the past, children were natural and willing apprentices to the lifestyle of their parents. There was a casual, tacitly understood integration of children into adult life. Parenting was not about expressing one's emotions and open communication. Parenting was about teaching the social value of teamwork to make survival easier. Family was about parent and child working side-by-side toward a common goal.

From barn-raising to threshing crews, parents taught by modeling. They modeled cooperation, as families and communities worked together to better provide for their families. Each family's social support network was understood, and taken for granted as an essential part of survival. As a community went, so went the individuals in each family within it. Children were apprentices to parents, learning the skills and values needed to survive and, hopefully, thrive.

American parents have deceived themselves that parenting is about giving kids attention—or even communication, for that matter. Our ancestors spent very little time playing with their children, and even less time building their self-esteem. To our ancestors, parenting was about teaching survival skills by example, and maintaining authority to ensure their family worked as a team. Rather than giving kids attention, parent and child simply worked many hours together for the good of the family. What they verbalized during that time together was not as important as the atmosphere—the vibe—between them. Rather than expressing deep emotions, parent and child may have been largely silent, but there was a calm, casual, simple emotional stability as they went about their chores together.

Let me underline the word *casual*. Don't get me wrong: Nobody wants to return to the Victorian era of "Children should be seen and not heard." I don't idealize the past, because it was not all roses: it used to be socially acceptable to beat one's children, and during the early Industrial Revolution, children were little more than illiterate slaves.

Parenting has indeed come a long way, but perhaps we have gone too far in the other direction. There must be a happy medium between Victorian times and the crazy intensity and hand-wringing of the modern parent-child relationship. Today, everything a child says or does is so *significant*. Parents attach an incredibly high importance to their child's every utterance, sand castle, report card, dance performance, and soccer game. We are constantly interpreting our child's behavior, comparing it to the checklist of how we *think* he or she should be doing. We over-think and over-analyze not only our child's every action, but our every reaction. Today's parents don't even realize how the air between us and our children is fraught with intensity and hand-wringing anxiety. We look at every issue so intensely that we may be creating more problems than we're solving—and creating an environment where we find exactly the things we fear the most for our children.

The buck stops here, and now. I hope this book has awakened you to just how much you are sacrificing in the name of raising perfect, trauma-free kids. Perhaps you thought you were the only one making such noble sacrifices. I hope you now see how in fact you have been sacrificing the health and well-being of your children and your spouse, as well as yourself.

And you are not alone. We have all been subjecting our children to friendly fire. We had the best of intentions, but somewhere along the line our stress levels hit critical mass, and we were no longer making a constructive contribution to the future of our children. Instead, we inadvertently touched off a chain reaction in the nervous systems of our children that led to anxiety, neurodevelopmental disorders, depression, autoimmune diseases, and a frenetic, hope-sucking, chaotic lifestyle that no one in their right mind could actually enjoy.

That's the bad news. The good news is that we can now ease back. We can do less, and socialize more with a clear conscience, because we have no choice. To have more fun and be more casual is, amazingly, the best thing we can do for our children.

The pendulum has swung too far. The human race went from laziness to craziness, and now we have to find a middle ground. We need to achieve a balance between making a living and having a life. We need to raise children while at the same time not dropping our marriage. Aristotle was right: all things in moderation. Until recently, we didn't even realize we had gone to an extreme. But now that we know, we can change for the better by doing less.

I understand how this book can be both confronting and overwhelming. If you're like most parents today, you're already plenty stressed out. And learning that your stress may be harming your child's health is just one more thing adding to that stress. But before you throw in the towel, remember why you are reading this book: to be the best parent you can be for your child and to find real-world solutions that can work for your family.

Parents have a right to know how they may be shooting their kids in the foot, so that they can change their lifestyle in a way that will improve their children's health in the long run. We also have to think of future generations. Since medical studies show that stress harms our children, we need to warn future parents so they can do better than our generation did. We can't simply keep this information secret because it might hurt the feelings of today's parents.

I believe it would actually be a relief to step out of the vicious circle we find ourselves in. Right now, we have convinced ourselves that we don't have time to socialize because our children's needs come first. But we need to realize the genuine, urgent medical imperative to manage our stress by relaxing and socializing. Consider this book a "doctor's note" that gives you permission to finally pursue hobbies that fulfill you, and to attend adult dinners and parties with a clear conscience.

Fortunately, there is a happy ending: have more fun! I hope that I have convinced you of the medical imperative to reduce stress. Now it's time to look at practical ways to do just that. This is one of those rare instances where change is going to feel good. Having fun will be a relief. Socializing more will be a civic duty. Let the fun begin...

PART THREE

Practical Strategies to Help You Raise Healthy Kids
by Relaxing and Socializing More

Chapter 12

How to Reduce Stress by Socializing More

This chapter offers practical strategies to improve our children's health by reducing our own stress. The best way to reduce our stress is to increase our "social grooming," so the following seven sections explain how to renew our relationships:

1) Getting Back to "Baseline"

2) Socializing More With Your Spouse

3) With Your Parents

4) With Your Siblings and Relatives

5) With Friends

6) With Work Colleagues

7) With Neighbors and Community

1) Get Back to "Baseline"

My wife loves yoga. She takes classes, and practices her own routine for 20 minutes before bed and 20 minutes when she gets up in the morning. I love talking with my wife after her yoga sessions, because she is so relaxed, exuberant, and quick to laugh. Any problems she has seem much smaller after she gets back in touch with her body and soul through yoga.

I consider yoga to be my wife's way of "returning to baseline." Think of "baseline" in the medical sense, like our baseline heart rate or our baseline levels of stress hormones when we are in a relaxed, cheerful mood. Every time we experience a stressful event, our stress levels rise from their baseline level. Hopefully, they can return to baseline before the next stressor comes along.

We all have ways of returning to baseline. Some people eat or drink too much, escape into TV, or dump their stress on their families by blaming or criticizing them. Others exercise, call a friend, read, pray, have sex, or take a nap.

The point is, you want to find ways of returning to baseline that benefit you and your loved ones. Things like yoga, meditation, and prayer tend to fill us with peace and hope. Reading can transform your brain from upset, fight-or-flight mode to thoughtful mode, because the act of interpreting those printed symbols on the page forces our brains into thoughtful, intellectual mode, which steals the thunder from our stress-response.

Many people talk about getting in touch with their emotions. I'm only interested in getting in touch with my stress response, because my stress response is at the root of all the negative emotions I want to reduce: anger is my fight response, which is triggered by my stress response. Fear is my flight response, which again is triggered by my stress response. Any feelings of anxiety or stress are of course also my stress response.

Although people talk about their myriad of emotions, the root of almost all our negative emotions is the stress response. Most people don't realize just how much the stress response governs our feelings, and our behavior. But if we can learn to control the stress response, we have learned to control most of our negative emotions.

If we say we're feeling anxious or stressed, those terms describe subjective feeling-states. But our stress response is concrete and physiological. A certain part of our brain triggers our fight-or-flight response and releases stress hormones into our bloodstream, such as adrenaline, cortisol, and other stress steroids. Scientists can measure and quantify our stress response.

So when you're criticizing or blaming your spouse, you likely are in fight-or-flight mode. Ditto for when you raise your voice. I'm not saying never do it. We're all human. But just understand that behavior for what it is—you're likely in fight-or-flight mode.

Another barometer for your stress levels may be your child's health or acting-out behavior. Whenever your child displays any symptom, take a moment and analyze what's been going on in your household in the past few days or weeks. You'll be surprised at how often you can find something between you and your spouse that may have affected those little sponges we call our children.

When you find yourself anxious and stressed, remind yourself that this is normal for everyone, everyday, and be grateful that you are aware of your anxiety because that empowers you. Most people stumble through their day lashing out at whichever poor soul happens to trigger their fight-or-flight response. You have the opportunity to recognize your anxiety and get back to baseline before anyone can trip the wire on your fight-or-flight response. That means less grief for both you and your loved ones.

Take a vacation every three months (and every day!)

Vacation means a complete change of pace, and that's a great way to get back to baseline. Stop kidding yourself that you don't have the time or money, or the kids can't miss school. Once your family has the memories of a couple of vacations under your belt, you'll be happily addicted to travel, and you'll take pleasure in daydreaming and looking forward to the next trip.

Better yet, let's bring back the old-fashioned Daily Vacation: lunch hour. Leaving your office for an hour every day gives your stress-response a chance to return to baseline. Instead of building stress over eight hours, you'll start over again after lunch and not get so wound up by quitting time.

2) *How to socialize more with your Spouse*

Knowledge is power. Penn State University's Prevention Research Center for the Promotion of Human Development has conducted studies showing that even a brief relationship-strengthening seminar before a baby is born can improve the well-being of both parents and child. These positive effects appear to be long-lasting, and are beneficial to normal families, as well as those considered high-risk.

If we can begin to recognize that blaming our loved ones is actually our fight-or-flight instincts in action, we can take it as a sure sign that we're anxious about something. When we begin to see our criticism as merely our anxiety talking, it empowers us to pause the action for a moment and ponder whether we're perceiving our spouses as objectively as we thought.

That shadow of a doubt, that sliver of uncertainty, is fantastic because it derails the auto-pilot of our instinctive reactions. Thinking trumps the fight-or-flight response in your brain. The fight-or-flight response never wonders: it simply reacts in a split second. But if we're wondering, we're thinking. If we're thinking, we're not governed by our instincts alone. And the more we're thinking, the more willful control we have over our behavior, to produce a more thoughtful response.

This awareness can be like seeing behind the curtain in *The Wizard of Oz*. Once we understand anxiety as the source of our drama in life, we can have more compassion for others. Whatever they do (as cruel or as dumb as it seems) is the best they can do, given the level of anxiety they are battling. So, we can spend less time trying to fix our loved ones, and more time trying to change ourselves—which is where real empowerment lies.

We tend to believe most of the drama in our relationships is caused by the allegedly "immature" spouses we married. But it's actually empowering to realize the enemy is within. Much of the conflict in our home and office is caused by our primal fight-or-flight instincts, which are triggered by our stress response. Once we understand how anxiety works within our brains, we can change some of our anxious overreactions into more thoughtful responses, taming the caveman within.

Of course, I can't feel my brain trigger the stress response, or count the number of stress hormones in my blood. But I can watch for certain flags in my behavior that indicate my stress response has kicked in. If I criticize my spouse, that's a red flag that I'm irritable, which means my stress levels are up. Sure, there are times my spouse does something wrong. But let's admit that our spouses sure tend to do a lot *more* wrong when we're irritable. Or, we can't help mentioning what they've done wrong when we're irritable. Why did we mention something this time, when in fact they've done that same, annoying thing many times before? Because our stress and irritability are up.

Marriage is a school for lovers, so contrary to popular belief, it's not about managing your partner. It's about managing your anxiety. This insight can help you accept yourself and your spouse as you are, for better or for worse, in sickness and in health. As my mother-in-law was fond of saying, "Marriage is not a correctional institution."

Learning to notice our animal instincts by using the thoughtful part of our brain can tame the caveman within, and bring more peace to us and our loved ones. You may never look at your family the same way again.

So, what are the practical solutions that parents can apply to their families? To raise healthy kids, relax and go for a walk with your spouse, have a drink with a friend, or call your mom! Here are some practical strategies:

Exercise together

If you make a daily, unbreakable date to maintain your waistline, it becomes an unbreakable date for your marriage as well. My wife and I have tried the "date night" thing so many times and it goes well for a month or so and then fades.

We have found that it's easier to discuss tough topics and get emotional when we are side by side on the treadmill or jogging down the street. It's easier to be emotional in motion.

If you have previously tried but failed to maintain a regular exercise program, having your spouse as an exercise partner may help you succeed. It's much easier to build an exercise habit if you have company while exercising, and you feel compelled to keep your promise to your partner. On many days, the only thing that gets me into my jogging clothes is my wife's presence. But once we're out there running together, I am always grateful to her for keeping me honest!

If you simply can't find the time or energy to exercise, then an evening stroll together can be highly beneficial. It becomes your daily time to "have a marriage," and even ten minutes of marital maintenance per day can make the difference between a healthy relationship and a marriage starving to death over ten years. Also, you will find that when you are outdoors under a big sky, any problems or stress you feel seem much smaller by comparison.

One of the best investments my wife and I ever made was a Gore-Tex rain suit from LL Bean, with waterproof shoes and gloves. Our outfits cost us about $300 each, but for over ten years, they have provided us the freedom to go "singing in the rain"!

Another gift to modern marriage is a walkie-talkie with a voice-activated switch, because it works like a high-tech baby monitor. After the kids fall asleep, set the monitor beside them and then take a stroll around your yard with your spouse. Stay close enough that, if a kid wakes up, you're never more than a 20-second sprint from them. Some people may be afraid to leave the kids sleeping, but you can probably hear more through this walkie-talkie than if you're watching TV downstairs.

Every night couples can enjoy 30 minutes of exercise, fresh air, and the chance to share what they're thinking, feeling, and dreaming.

"Let the Air Out" of Your Inner Dialogues

Comedian George Carlin had a hilarious routine in which he articulated what everyone is thinking, but no one dares to say out loud. He called it The Secret News:

> *Good Evening Ladies and Gentlemen, It's Time For the Secret News.*
> *Sshh.*
> *Here's the secret news:*
> *All people are afraid.*
> *No one knows what they're doing.*
> *Everything is getting worse.*

Some people deserve to die.

Your money is worthless.

No one is properly dressed.

At least one of your children will disappoint you.

The system is rigged.

Your house will never be completely clean.

All teachers are incompetent.

There are people who really dislike you.

Nothing is as good as it seems.

Things don't last.

No one is paying attention.

The country is dying.

God doesn't care.

Sshhhhhh.....

Have you ever noticed how each morning, as you get ready to go to work, the number of tasks, problems, and worries you face seems almost overwhelming? You may find great comfort in learning that evolution has programmed all humans to worry in the morning.

Scientists have documented a spike in stress hormones that each of us has when we wake up in the morning. Presumably, this extra rush of adrenaline evolved to help us wake up and get a jump on predators, by anticipating danger and organizing ourselves to fight, flee, or protect our offspring.

Unfortunately these days, as we shower and prepare breakfast, we don't feel limber and ready to fight off a saber-toothed tiger. Instead, we feel anxious and overwhelmed as our adrenaline-stoked inner dialogue blows all of our weaknesses and problems out of proportion, and we often believe we are the only ones who feel this way while everyone else is feeling confident and courageous.

You may be relieved to discover that everyone has these morning floods of stress hormones, and everyone has those feelings of being overwhelmed: that's why the highest incidence of heart attacks is on Monday morning. But you can find great relief in a simple, effective strategy to ease your beleaguered mind in the morning.

As you are dressing or putting on your make-up, tell your spouse it's time for your daily "Letting the Air Out," and then dig around in your mind to find out the inner dialogues causing you the most grief that day. (This technique is similar to Julia Cameron's "Morning Pages" exercise for artists.) Think of your inner dialogue as a big balloon that is only getting bigger with the morning's stress. When you articulate your inner dialogue, you let some of the air out of it. Most of our inner dialogues seem rather silly when we say them out loud, and they certainly seem less powerful because we are facing them head-on.

"Bella," a mother of three from Los Angeles, shared this success story:

> *I think that "Letting the Air Out" works equally well on a morning run with friends....and can help you build your community as well. I have a great running group of 5 women and we run at 5:30 in the morning, 3-4 days a week. It's the most cathartic part of my day, always, because we talk about everything and anything. And it's true that, often, just verbalizing quells the fear...I think also that a key component to my successful marriage, at least, is that my husband is NOT the key to all my emotional happiness. My running friends and coffee friends and lunch friends bear some of it as well – as I do for them.*

The act of speaking your inner dialogue out loud to another person is cathartic, because you are converting a stress-soaked feeling into a thoughtful statement. When your morning stress response is in high gear, it's easy to kick into fight-or-flight because your fearful primal instincts are running the show. But the act of thinking through what you are feeling and then articulating it actually employs the frontal lobe, that part of the brain which is most evolved in humans and houses higher-order cognitive functions. To think about, become conscious of, and voice our feelings is to organize feelings into thoughts. And verbal statements are much easier to analyze than amorphous feelings. We can then weigh our statements for evidence or examples, and we may often find we were exaggerating the threat.

Usually, just the simple act of saying it out loud lets a lot of air out of the "balloon" of our inner dialogues, so we have nothing to lose and everything to gain by speaking them out loud every morning before work. You may notice that your inner dialogues are often the same each day. That's normal. We all have a few of those destructive thought patterns, and acknowledging them reduces their power over us.

It's important that, when you listen to your partner, you simply *listen*, which is harder than it sounds. Most of us are sorely tempted to advise, correct, or coach our spouses. That's not the goal of this exercise. The goal is simply to be heard, and the act of speaking freely is cathartic. Resist the temptation to coach your spouse unless they ask for it specifically.

So try letting the air out of your balloons tomorrow morning for three minutes. You may find this exercise not only connects you with your spouse, but also makes your morning go a little smoother!

Realize that "The Grass Is Not Greener"

My wife and I are certain that we would be divorced by now if it were not for this insight: I am not superior to my spouse, and vice versa. We have the same level of immaturity, we just manifest it in different ways. Let me explain:

If you made every married person drink a truth serum, you would discover a secret belief many of us have that we've "outgrown" our mate, and we could be happy if we just started over with "the right person THIS time." But we're kidding ourselves, because as I have stated before, the divorce rate for second marriages is 60 percent, and 73 percent for third marriages.

The solution is to realize that the grass would NOT be greener with someone else, and here's why: We have to remember that humans are animals, with primal mating instincts. When we fall in love, that primal **chemistry** we feel is actually Mother Nature's way of scoping out our ideal mate. We instinctively search for a mate with the same level of anxiety. Anxiety is a survival instinct, because back in our caveman days, it helped us anticipate danger and trigger our fight-or-flight response.

For example, if you were a bit jumpy and overreacted to every noise you hear in the bushes, but your mate lounged in the sun even as the lion roared nearby, you wouldn't last long together. Back then, you might say the couple who fights-or-flees together stays together—and reproduces.

So Mother Nature doesn't lie. The reason you felt chemistry for your mate in the first place is because you both have the same level of anxiety.

So the next time you're feeling more "mature" than your spouse who overreacts to everything, just remember you both have the same level of anxiety—you just may show it in different ways. If you bear in mind that you have the same levels of anxiety, then you can accept your spouse as he or she is, and settle down to create the best marriage possible.

Highlight and Lowlight

Want a one-minute instant Intimacy-Builder?

When you both get home from work, while changing or preparing dinner, share your highlight and "lowlight" of the day with your spouse. Rather than saying, "I enjoyed my walk from the train to the office," try to focus on one moment in time. For example, "I was walking to work when I noticed a lovely oak in all its fall colors. I felt one of those 'happy to be alive' moments!"

Sharing the lowlight of our day feels good because if we commiserate with our partner, we won't feel so alone in our suffering. Instead of muttering, "I had a crummy day at work today," be specific: "When I borrowed the office projector for my presentation, the receptionist grilled me about how long I'd keep it, as if I were some kind of selfish jerk who hogs everything. It really ticked me off."

Sharing one's highlight and lowlight may sound simple, but it can instantly create a space for being fully present to each other. This creates a sense of shared intimacy and preempts future problems.

"Desiree," a mother of three from Washington state, related this success story to me:

> We do this every night at our family dinners. We call it "best and worst" and everyone around the table has to say his or her best and worst, no exceptions. What's amazing to me is that it's often the kids who

initiate this.

Make a weekly appointment for sex

Once humans have sex with a partner, we instinctively want to have more sex with that partner.

Even if you don't feel like having sex with your spouse, you may find that, after a couple of times, the desire returns. Hormones such as oxytocin and vasopressin help mates to bond in the sexual act, and this primal bond can smooth the waters of many marriages.

3) How to Socialize More with Your Parents

Sexless couples who wonder why they don't talk much anymore might take a look at their relationship with their own parents. It turns out that people who distance themselves from their parents also tend to distance themselves from their spouses. If you have trouble getting along with your parents, you may think it's the best solution to move away from your family of origin and distance yourself. This may seem to keep the peace with "those unreasonable relatives," but you're hurting yourself and your kids.

In Europe and developing nations, where three generations of a family often live in close proximity, divorce and addictions are lower, and mental health is higher.

There are plenty of creative ways to stay in contact with even the most difficult parents. Below are some examples:

If you cannot bear to even be in the same room with your parent, writing letters is a great way to stay in touch. People mistakenly think they have to fully express their pain or seek reconciliation with the parent. Not at all. All they have to do to reap the benefits of lower stress is to make regular contact. You can write letters, email, or make phone calls that talk about the weather. You can send birthday cards or small gifts on the parent's special day. You can be sure to visit that parent with your family or other relatives, such that you are never alone in the room.

A visit doesn't have to be that traumatic, since you need not have any lofty goal in your relationship. What makes contact with difficult parents hard is that we have this popular, mistaken belief that you must create some kind of sweeping, cathartic confrontation. This is not the case. All you need to receive benefit is to be in touch. It doesn't even matter if they don't reply to your writing, or return your phone calls. It's your pro-active effort to be in touch, knowing that you did your best to reach out, that confers the benefit on your psyche.

For example, take James and Gail from New York (not their real names). "Before, my tombstone could have read, 'My life was my husband's fault,'" Gail says. "But then I noticed that in my relationship with my parents, I was polite but distant—often just going through the motions with them. And I eventually realized I was doing the same thing with James."

"I felt tremendous relief, because now I knew I didn't have to put my kids and myself through the hell of a divorce," Gail remembers. "Instead of focusing on what was wrong with James, I focused on noticing when I was in fight-or-flight mode. Now, we make up much more quickly after an argument, and I don't carry all that bitterness because I know it's nothing personal, just our fight-or-flight running the show. And it's a bonus that I stopped going through the motions with my parents, and actually *engaged* them as real friends with real conversations about what's really going on in my life. Now, I'm amazed to say that I actually look forward to time with my mom!"

I have heard about an institution that cared for girls who were victims of abuse from their parents. The staff started a new program to provide chaperones to those girls who wished to visit their parents but were afraid to do so alone. The staff noticed that the grade point averages of these girls increased markedly after they began visiting their estranged parents. It didn't seem to matter what was actually said; it was merely the contact that had a beneficial effect.

Of course, apologies and forgiveness are the ideal, but much healing can take place by the simple act of making contact. A monthly letter or weekly phone call is much better than nothing at all.

Keep the Sabbath

When a couple force themselves to forgo work, errands or shopping for one day of the week, it doesn't leave them much to focus on—except relationships. Many couples find that socializing with friends or relatives re-invigorates their marriage as well. Humans have forgotten we are social animals, and socializing one day a week lowers our stress levels and re-charges our batteries with laughter and vitality.

Sure, we've all been caught up in that vicious cycle where we believe we're so busy that to "lose" one day a week will make us fall impossibly far behind in everything we have to do. But we may be kidding ourselves, because many Jews and Christians known for keeping the Sabbath are also quite successful in terms of career or quality of life.

Keep the Sabbath, and make that day your "relationship day," when you reach out by writing or calling your siblings and relatives. A Jewish friend of mine remarked,

> *A whole day is too much for our family to dedicate to relationships. We simply practice a Shabbat dinner. It puts us back in touch with both our family and our roots.*

4) How to Socialize More with your Siblings and Relatives

Put all their birthdays, anniversaries, and special days on your digital calendar, so that a reminder automatically pops up. Few things win you more good will than remembering people on their special days. Whether we like it or not, the people who contact us on our special days become a sort of litmus test for who our *true* friends are, so setting up reminders is an easy way to gain a lot of good will from family and friends.

The more relatives you spend time with, the healthier your kids. As Dan Buettner pointed out in Chapter 1, statistics show that "the way socialization works, we get more satisfaction retroactively by socializing with our parents than anybody else." Our family is our primal "herd" in society, and how we get along with our herd is a model for how we get along in greater society as well. It's no coincidence that, generally speaking, those who get along with their families tend to get along with their co-workers and neighbors.

I'm not glossing over the challenges of getting along with some of our family members. I'm simply saying that the effort you put into improving those relationships pays dividends. So, organize a family reunion, or a family cruise. Both you and your children will benefit.

5) *How to Socialize More with your Friends*

Parents can easily meet many other parents through their children's school events and after-school activities. Yet ironically, few parents can actually find the time to schedule a dinner together because they are so engrossed with shuttling their children to activities, or giving them more attention.

In fact, the best gift you can give your child is to have more adult friends. The more friends you have, the healthier your kids. This ought to give you more incentive to pick up the phone and carve out a time in your week to get together, either with or without your kids.

A great option is to start a supper club. It means each family prepares dinner one time less each week or month, and it's also a lot of fun. You'll notice how thrilled the kids are to all get together and play downstairs or outside while the parents relax over a drink before dinner—just like our parents used to do! Or if you prefer, a Sunday brunch can be much easier to schedule and people might be more relaxed then.

6) *How to Socialize More with your Work Colleagues*

The more you build community, both at work and in your neighborhood, the healthier and happier your kids will be.

You spend so much time in your workplace that you want it to be as socially fulfilling as possible.

You may recall one of author Dan Buettner's secrets to happiness, mentioned in Chapter 1: "the biggest determinant of whether or not you'll like your job is if you have a best friend there, more so than how much you're paid, so proactively make sure you have good friends there. One way I assert doing that is: Be the one who organizes happy hour."

7) *How to Socialize More with your Neighbors and Community*

Join a service organization.

Our family loves Boy and Girl Scouts because the kids have a blast socializing while they do community service projects. They come to associate helping others with having fun, so it's like programming your child to become a good citizen while enjoying the process!

Organize an annual block party at the beginning of summer. It brings all the families back into contact who have been "hibernating" indoors over the winter, and when you all see how much fun you had together, then over the summer many invitations will blossom from this original party!

What I Most Want You To Take Away From This Book

It may seem too good to be true, but this book gives you permission to *have more fun*. No, this book actually *insists* that you have more fun—your children's health (not to mention your marriage) depends on it.

Perhaps humans have evolved a little *too* much lately: Our ancestors used to take *siestas*. Then, we introduced the 9-to-5 work day. Then, we eliminated the lunch hour and started working Saturdays. After that, we allowed stores to stay open on Sundays, and then we started working on Sundays, too, even if we worked from home. In recent generations, humans have proved that we have an infinite capacity to do more work.

To what end?

Once upon a time, our parents or grandparents were too busy working or socializing to babysit us, so we had to entertain ourselves. But now, we actually do our kids' homework for them, and we even do all their household chores so they can fit in all their homework, sports, and music practices.

We need to step off the treadmill. The term "rat race" may have been coined in the 1950's, but it has never been more true than today.

There is always more we could be doing for our careers, and more we could be doing for our children. We are more than willing to sacrifice our own friendships, hobbies, and even our marriages in order to pay ever more attention to our children. Where does it all stop?

I'm hoping the buck stops here. People need to get the message that stress is by far the most toxic thing in our environment, and no single toxin impacts our children's health more. We need to take a stand for relaxing and socializing.

I'm also hoping that our frenzied guilt and self-blame can stop here. You shouldn't blame yourself for problems your child has. Most parents have the best of intentions—we simply didn't know how we were harming our kids, so we shouldn't blame ourselves for ignorance. This book may be the first time many of these issues were raised for you. So, you are not to blame, but you can always improve things, no matter what your starting point!

Perhaps the best news is that genetics are not nearly as "set in stone" as we thought. If we can become aware of our stress and reduce our anxiety, we can actually reverse some gene-switching, so everybody wins.

Another wonderful thing about self-awareness of our anxiety is that it gives you *compassion*. Now you understand how every single person you meet is *up against it*. They're struggling with the same anxiety, the same demons in their heads, as you. We spend most of the day, every day, *overreacting* to each other. And most folks out there don't even *realize* that's what they're doing, and they *certainly* have no idea how to change it. That's why they seek solace in medication, alcohol, an affair, or throwing themselves into their children. They desperately want relief, but don't know how else to get it.

But *you* know. It's a lifelong process, but at least now you have a clear route, one that you chose yourself. You know that your ticket to relief is learning to monitor your anxiety levels, and manage your fight-or-flight response. You also know you can reduce your stress levels by interacting more with your friends, parents, and siblings.

From now on, you have a direction, and you no longer have to learn from trial and error. You know that every ounce of effort you put toward socializing and reducing stress will pay dividends and have a ripple effect through all your relationships. How's *that* for motivation? You'll no longer be flailing in the dark, hoping things get better (or that at least they don't get *worse*). You now know how to make slow, steady progress. And slow, steady progress is exactly what I wish for you.

I'd love to hear from you as soon as you close this book. You can reach me at David@DavidArthurCode.com. I'm interested in hearing your stories, and which of my book's points resonated most strongly with you, as well as how you plan to apply the lessons of this book in your own family. Thank you for joining me on this bold, hopeful journey, and I wish you many friends and much fun!

APPENDIX 1

Further Evidence Of The Mind-Body Connection Between Parent And Child

In 2008 Dr. Audrey Saftlas, of the Department of Epidemiology at University of Iowa reviewed the evidence of the impact of prenatal stress in both animals and people. Based on 60 human and 43 animal studies, Dr. Saftlas concluded that the overall evidence suggested prenatal stress is a strong risk factor for disorders including ADHD.

There are also many studies suggesting that stress during pregnancy has a detrimental effect on babies. For example, one study in Belgium measured the anxiety levels of 71 pregnant women, and then tested their children once they had reached eight years of age. The children of moms who were rated high in anxiety during their pregnancy were 22 percent more likely to have ADHD, even after researchers eliminated other possible contributing factors like whether the moms smoked or had low education levels. This study and others suggest that pregnant women who experienced stressful events during their pregnancy had an increased risk of giving birth to babies who would later develop social and learning problems, including autism.

Dr. Alan Ward was working at Thomas Jefferson Hospital in

Philadelphia and the Institute for Juvenile Research in Chicago when he published a stunningly prophetic article on autism in 1990. Long before other researchers spoke of fetal programming or epigenetics in conjunction with autism, Dr. Ward found previous studies documenting, in his words, an "association between prenatal maternal anxiety focused upon ongoing personal tensions in the marriage and the later development of significant numbers of childhood psychopathologies and behavior disturbances." He wondered if prenatal anxiety and relationship tension might also apply to offspring who developed autism.

But his research indicated that the link wasn't as simple as "stressed women give birth to autistic babies," and this study from Yale agrees. Rather, Dr. Ward suspected that both stress and lack of a satisfactory marriage and social support network were risk factors for babies with neurodevelopmental disorders.

Indeed, Dr. Ward's study with 59 mothers at Thomas Jefferson Hospital found evidence to support what had been known as a folk wisdom or "an old wives' tale" in many cultures, namely, that stress during pregnancy was linked to offspring with mental disorders, and specifically autism. He was one of the first to advocate early intervention in pregnancies where emotional and relationship stress were evident.

Dr. Fred Previc concurs with Dr. Ward. Before becoming a lecturer at Texas A&M University, Dr. Previc spent more than 25 years as a researcher in cognitive neuroscience and aviation psychology at the U. S. Air Force Research Lab and for the Southwest Research Institute, and he has authored over 70 peer-reviewed papers and two books.

In the journal *Medical Hypotheses* he notes that the incidence of autism has increased ten-fold in the past three decades, in industrialized but not in developing countries. This increase cannot be explained by better diagnosis or genetics alone, since many autistic children have no history of the disorder in their family tree.

Dr. Previc believes that epigenetics plays a big role in neurodevelopmental disorders, and factors such as nutrition, drugs, and especially psychosocial stress are important. He writes that, "Mothers of autistic children have been shown to be nearly 10 times as likely as mothers with normal children to experience family discord during pregnancy."

One prominent prenatal stress researcher is Dr. Marta Weinstock. She is a professor of medicine at Hebrew University in Jerusalem. In our conversations, I found it charming that she takes great pains never to refer to children as "kids." Having grown up in England with the Queen's English, she still associates the word "kid" with young goats.

Dr. Weinstock's review of medical literature on prenatal stress notes that, when researchers stress a pregnant mother rat in the lab, her offspring go on to display ADHD-like behavior. Dr. Weinstock hypothesized that this pattern was because the stressed mother had more stress hormones in her blood, which were crossing over her placenta to affect her offspring's development.

To test her hypothesis, Dr. Weinstock removed the adrenal glands of the mothers of these rats. Since adrenaline is a stress hormone, she assumed that, if the mother rat had no adrenaline to cross the placenta, she would not produce offspring with ADHD-like behavior. This proved to be the case.

However, if a researcher then injects stress hormones into the womb of a rat whose adrenal glands have been removed, once again her offspring will exhibit symptoms of ADHD. Dr. Weinstock concludes that maternal stress hormones affect the neural development of the fetus to determine the behavior of the offspring.

In 2010, Rosalind Wright studied the level of immune response cells in the cord blood of 557 babies born of largely minority mothers under considerable socioeconomic stress. She concluded that prenatal stress altered the babies' immune responses (specifically, their CBMC cell production), which made them prone to develop allergic or asthmatic reactions as children.

In a recent review of the medical research, experts at the University of Texas Department of Obstetrics find that the incidence of asthma continues to increase every year, something genes or toxic exposures cannot fully explain. Their own findings agree: there is a link between asthma and allergies and the predictive adaptive response, with stress as a significant risk factor.

A number of studies suggest that premature birth is also linked to neurodevelopmental difficulties in the child. For example, Dr. Neil Marlow has been the Chair of Neonatology at University of Nottingham since 1997. He and Dr. Sam Johnson published a study of 219 babies who were born in1995, after less than 26 weeks of gestation. These babies were tested again at 11 years of age. When compared to 153 peers who were born at full-term, these 219 preterm babies were four times more likely to develop ADHD and eight times more likely to develop autism.

Dr. Kate Scott, a professor of Psychological Medicine at the University of Otago in New Zealand, had been reading the same medical literature, and she questioned whether asthma was linked to mental health disorders, or perhaps was simply a product of childhood adversity.

Her analysis of data on over 18,000 people showed that childhood adversity made people 49 percent more likely to develop asthma as adults. She also found that childhood anxiety disorders increased the likelihood of adult asthma by 67 percent. These results were important because they showed that anxiety alone was a risk factor for asthma, regardless of the number of "hard-knocks" one had received as a child.

APPENDIX 2

Dr. Jiong Li: Prenatal Stress Increases the Odds of ADHD, but Not Autism?

Dr. Jiong Li is a researcher at the Department of Epidemiology at Denmark's Aarhus University. He and his colleagues collected certain data from pre-existing birth and health statistics on all babies born in Denmark between 1978 and 2003, an approach similar to Dr. Kinney's in the Louisiana Storm study.

Nevertheless, Dr. Li's conclusions differed from those of the Louisiana storm study. Instead, Dr. Li concluded that prenatal stress, as caused by the loss of a loved one before or during pregnancy, did not increase the odds of a child being born with autism.

However, there are two strange twists here:

1) A closer look at Dr. Li's raw data shows that they look strikingly similar to the data in Dr. Kinney's study; and

2) In a separate study, Dr. Li interpreted similar data from the same Danish babies to conclude that prenatal stress increased the odds of children being born with ADHD.

So, why the difference? How can Dr. Li's data disagree with Dr.

Kinney in one instance, yet agree in another? Many experts believe Dr. Li factored out too many other factors that affect a mother's stress levels, like her social support network or any history of psychological problems. This is an important issue, and merits a closer look:

Dr. Li's goal with the Danish birth statistics from 1978 to 2003 was to find out how many babies were born to a mother who had lost a loved one during pregnancy, because losing a loved one should be a big stressor, and therefore one would expect these bereaved women to give birth to more children with problems. Take, for example, the experience of Jennifer Hutchings of San Diego, whose son, Joey, has ADHD. She wonders if her grandmother's death contributed to her son's ailment:

> *My grandmother died unexpectedly two months before my due date. She had helped raise me, and we had been particularly close. I often felt closer to her than to my mom. She was a passenger in a car accident and suffered internal injuries that she was too frail to recover from…*
>
> *I felt tremendously lucky to have had her so long, but the grief was very difficult to deal with. I was afraid to really let myself grieve, as the pain and loss were so strong I felt as though I might never be able to stop crying once I started, so I threw myself into the preparations for her memorial service, to be held a month after her death.*

Returning to Dr. Li's study in Denmark: Of almost 1.5 million children born during those 25 years, just over 37,000 babies were born to mothers who had lost a loved one in the two years preceding their birth. When they collected data on those 37,000 babies, Li's team found a higher incidence of autism, ADHD and other disorders. Not surprising.

But here's the shocker: Dr. Li chose to exclude portions of his own data.

Dr. Li's data was very much in keeping with Dr. Kinney's Louisiana Storm study, and dozens of other studies suggesting that the high stress of bereavement was linked to neurodevelopmental disorders. However, when Dr. Li analyzed his data, he chose to exclude some of his own statistics which he had collected. Why would he do that? Let's look a little deeper into the numbers.

Dr. Li's data even agreed with Drs. Kinney and Beversdorf's conclusion about the *timing* of stress, i.e., *when* a pregnant mother lost a loved one during her pregnancy, was key. For example, Dr. Li found that, if a pregnant woman lost a loved one during her first trimester, she was 50 percent more likely to give birth to an autistic child. And shockingly, if pregnant women lost a loved one during their *second* trimester, the rate of children who would be born with autism rose to a stunning 94 percent! This number went down a bit for women who lost loved ones during their third trimesters; they had a 63 percent chance of giving birth to an autistic child— still high, but not as high as the second trimester.

But here's the twist: Dr. Li got the same results with his data as Dr. Kinney, but he chose to interpret his data differently. In other words, he chose to factor out other stressors, such as the mother's psychiatric history or the quality of her social support network. Dr. Li would argue that factoring out the mother's psychiatric history or the quality of her marriage would make his results more accurate, because he is considering the impact of each stressor separately: i.e., bereavement as distinct from marital problems, as distinct from the mother's psychiatric history.

But many experts believe he may have factored out too many things, because many of these stressors contribute to each other, and one risk factor amplifies the effects of another.

For example, many studies have already concluded that, if a woman has mental illness or relationship problems with her partner, these issues already indicate she has a high level of stress. If the death of her loved one is added to this high stress, it will likely *compound* the risk of her giving birth to an autistic child.

So, if a pregnant woman already has relationship problems even before her mother dies, one may assume that she will not get the kind of support she needs from her husband, and therefore this will drive her stress levels even higher as she grieves. If we add mental illness to the mix, the effect would presumably be even more dramatic.

Some experts disagree with Dr. Li's interpretation of his data because we cannot simply consider mental illness, relationship problems, and death of a loved one as three independent risk factors, each one contributing separately to an expectant mother's stress levels.

The interplay of these risk factors is the main reason why many experts disagree with Dr. Li's interpretation. One cannot easily disentangle bereavement stress from relationship stress or the anxiety of mental illness, although Dr. Nicole Talge of Michigan State University's Department of Epidemiology tried. She estimates in her review of medical studies that prenatal anxiety accounts for at least 15 percent of the risk of giving birth to an autistic child, based on several different studies. She writes, "If we were able to substantially reduce stress in pregnant women, such findings suggest that this may have an important effect on social and cognitive developmental outcomes (page 252)."

However, perhaps the strongest evidence refuting Dr. Li's interpretation is another study done using almost exactly the same Danish birth and health statistics. This study was done by Dr. William Eaton, who is both Chair of the Department of Mental Health and a professor at Johns Hopkins Medical School. In 2005 he teamed up with Dr. Heidi Larsson (who also works at Dr. Li's Aarhus University) to publish an article on the risk factors for autism.

They studied the records of 698 babies born in Denmark between 1972 and 1999 who went on to develop autism. Drs. Weaton and Larsson also found a very high incidence of autistic children born to anxious mothers with either mood disorders or mental illness. Parents with a mood disorder were almost three times more likely to give birth to autistic children, and parents with psychiatric history (i.e., mental illness, such as schizophrenia) were almost three-and-a-half times more likely to bear children with autism.

It also is important to note that Dr. Li himself did another, parallel study on the effects of maternal bereavement on children who developed ADHD. Mothers who lost a loved one from up to six months before their pregnancy were 47 percent more likely to give birth to a child who would develop ADHD, but mothers who lost a loved one *during* their pregnancy were more than twice as likely to birth a child who would go on to develop ADHD.

Dr. Li's ADHD statistics line up well with the 2002 study by Dr. Vivette Glover of Imperial College in London and Dr. Tom O'Connor of the University of Rochester, who studied 7,000 children over a period of years, and found that expectant mothers who suffered from anxiety or depression had double the risk of their child having behavioral problems at age four.

So, if so many studies, including Dr. Li's ADHD study, have found a link between prenatal stress and child ailments, how do we explain Dr. Li's conflicting conclusion regarding autism? Why the disparity?

It is important to note that Dr. Li's study included every mother who had lost a loved one even before becoming pregnant, for a period up to almost two years before birth. Most studies limit their time frame to gestation, and some periods of gestation, like the second trimester, appear to be more vulnerable to stress than others.

Acknowledgments

Like many writers, I also am struck by the irony of my name alone listed on the cover as author. I'd like to acknowledge some of my "co-authors," without whom I could not have created this work.

The following people believed in me long before this book became a reality: Alexis Rizzuto, Ana Vargas, Barbara Code, Christine Bell, David and Linda Masson, Douglas Allen, Jaak Panksepp, Joshua Burek, Katherine Armstrong, Kelly Bozanic, Lew Logan, Penny Wark, Ross Garber, and Tim Leslie.

These people gave me valuable support and guidance once I was underway: Aaron Shepherd, Adam Shayne, Alan Finder, Brian Code, Brucie Serene, Charles Forelle, Daniel Akst, Darby Saxbe, David Beversdorf, David Lauter, David Sherry, Emma Hess, Farrah Ferguson, Fred Previc, Jean Booth, Jen DeVore, Jim Serene, JoAnn Foley De-Fiore, Judith Warner, Julia Pimsleur, Kate Freeman, Kevin McGarry, Kim Screen, Mark Cunningham, Martin Beiser, Matt Heimer, Michael McCoy, Michael Meaney, Moshe Szyf, Neela Banerjee, Patrick Davies, Richard Wall, Rodney Sepich, Sharon Begley,

Suzanne King, Valerie Hu, Victoria Bosch, Vivette Glover, Warren Code, and Wendy Cox.

The team at CreateSpace and Kindle have been amazing: Libby Johnson McKee, James Dickinson, John Rieck, Brian Mitchell, Juliana and Julie.

These people are my mentors, who have stood by me through thick and thin: Gerald McKelvey, Jamie Callaway, Kathleen Kerr, Lloyd Prator, Roberta Gilbert, Robert Laird, Ward Ewing, Larry Hofer, Andy Luke, Mike Peters, George Werner, Masaro Miyajima, and Ric Connors.

My own two children are now old enough to take interest in my work, and their perspectives and insights delight me.

I want to thank my mom for giving me the gift of life. Dad, it's lonely down here without you.

My wife is not only my inspiration and the "Lennon" of our Lennon & McCartney creative duo. She is also the greatest gift God has given me.

ENDNOTES

Dear Reader,

In an effort to save a few trees, I have identified each citation by only its title and "PMID," which stands for PubMed ID. PubMed is the US National Library of Medicine at the National Institute of Health. A Google search of "PMID: 12345678" will bring up each article.

INTRODUCTION

xii   *described "a striking emotional distance*: Family Therapy in Clinical Practice by Murray Bowen (Northvale, NJ: Jason Aronson Press, 1978), pp. 21, 27

xiii   *Asthma now affects 1 child in 10:* http://www.cdc.gov/VitalSigns/Asthma/

xiv   *as does ADHD:* "1 in 10 kids in U.S. has ADHD, new study," MSNBC.com

xiv   *autism is 1 out of 110 children*: http://www.cdc.gov/ncbddd/features/counting-autism.html

xiv   *autism affects 1 of every 88*: http://www.thenhf.com/article.php?id=1877

xiv   *1 of every 88 of military families*: "Wartime military deployment and increased pediatric mental and behavioral health complaints," PMID: 21059715

xiv   *Silicon Valley the rate*: "The Geek Syndrome," www.Wired.com

xiv   *I want parents to see the urgent*: "Epigenetic Vestiges of Early Developmental Adversity: Childhood Stress Exposure and DNA Methylation in Adolescence," PMID: 21883162

xiv   *urgent medical imperative*: http://www.med.wisc.edu/news-events/news/

parents-stress-leaves-mark-on-dna-of-children/32279

xiv   *Contrary to popular belief:* "Surprisingly, Family Time Has Grown," *New York Times*, April 5, 2010

CHAPTER 1: TODAY'S EPIDEMIC OF STRESS AND CHILD DISORDERS

2   *A 2005 German study:* "Association between life stress during pregnancy and infant crying in the first six months postpartum: a prospective longitudinal study," PMID: 16472948

2   *Danish study of mothers:* "Psychosocial distress during pregnancy and the risk of infantile colic," PMID: 12892160

2   *A 2007 study:* "Antenatal maternal stress and long-term effects on child neurodevelopment: how and why?" PMID: 17355398

2   *A 2008 Harvard study:* "Chronic caregiver stress and IgE expression, allergen-induced proliferation, and cytokine profiles in a birth cohort predisposed to atopy," PMID: 15208584

2   *Rosalind Wright, states:* "Mother's prenatal stress predisposes their babies to asthma and allergy," e! Science News, May 18, 2008

2   *A 2009 Australian study:* "Mothers' anxiety during pregnancy is associated with asthma in their children," PMID: 19348924

2   *A 2008 Harvard review:* "Prenatal Stress And Risk For Autism," PMCID: PMC2632594

2   *A 2009 British study agrees:* "Prenatal stress and neurodevelopment of the child: focus on the HPA axis and role of the placenta," PMID: 19546565

2   *A 2008 Australian study:* "Early childhood aetiology of mental health problems: a longitudinal population-based study," PMID: 18665879

3   *A 2007 New Zealand study:* "Is later obesity programmed in utero?" PMID: 17691929

3   *A 2010 Danish study:* "Prenatal Stress Exposure Related to Maternal Bereavement and Risk of Childhood Overweight," PMCID: PMC2912844

3   *A 2002 UCLA study:* "Risky Families: Family Social Environments and the Mental and Physical Health of Offspring," PMID: 11931522

3   *One study analyzed the health:* "Continued exposure to maternal distress in early life is associated with an increased risk of childhood asthma," PMID: 17932381

3   *but research is showing that us not the case:* "Genetic Heritability and Shared Environmental Factors Among Twin Pairs With Autism," PMID: 21727249, and "Is Autism, at Least in Part, a Disorder of Fetal Programming?" PMID: 21730328

3   *lag far behind recent scientific research:* "Behavioral epigenetics," PMID: 21615751

3   *nearly 6,000 British children:* "Mothers' anxiety during pregnancy is associated with asthma in their children," PMID: 19348924

3   *3,000 California children:* "Parental stress and childhood wheeze in a prospective cohort study" PMID: 18446597

3   *Another study of 4,400 children in 2005:* "Psychological stress may induce diabetes-related autoimmunity in infancy," PMID: 15677781

4   *A 2011 Stanford twin study:* "Genetic Heritability and Shared Environmental Factors Among Twin Pairs With Autism," PMID: 21727249

4   *autism than is widely assumed:* "Is Autism, at Least in Part, a Disorder of Fetal Programming?" PMID: 21730328

4   *children of stressed parents get sick more often:* "The associations between psychosocial stress and the frequency of illness, and innate and adaptive immune function in children," PMID: 18308510

4   *suffer from more chronic health problems:* "Risky Families: Family Social Environments and the Mental and Physical Health of Offspring," PMID: 11931522

4   *how stressed-out we have become:* "Adapting to College Life In an Era of Heightened Stress," *New York Times*, August 06, 2000

5   *overreactive stress response can result in illness:* "Brain Is a Co-Conspirator in a Vicious Stress Loop," *New York Times*, August 17, 2009

6   *Dr. Dennis Kinney writes:* "Prenatal stress and risk for autism," PMCID: PMC2632594

9   *She found that more than five times:* "Birth cohort increases in psychopathology among young Americans, 1938-2007: A cross-temporal meta-analysis of the MMPI," PMID: 19945203

9   *we neglect the "social grooming":* "Social modulation of stress responses," PMID: 12954434

9   *improves our health and reduces:* "Neuroendocrine perspectives on social attachment and love," PMID: 9924738

10   *stressed-out we have become:* "Adapting to College Life In an Era of

Heightened Stress," *New York Times*, August 06, 2000

10   *as Dr. Jean Twenge writes:* "The age of anxiety? Birth cohort change in anxiety and neuroticism, 1952-1993," PMID: 11138751

11   *Many researchers in various other institutes have come to the same conclusion:* "Age-cohort changes in the lifetime occurrence of depression and other mental disorders," PMID: 8436687
"Increasing rates of depression," PMID: 2648043
"National patterns in antidepressant medication treatment," PMID: 19652124
"Why is there so much depression today? The waxing of the individual and the waning of the commons," http://psycnet.apa.org/psycinfo/1991-97018-001
"Further Examining the American Dream: Differential Correlates of Intrinsic and Extrinsic Goals," by Kasser, Tim; Ryan, Richard M.

11   *said they had no one to confide in:* "Lonely Planet," Newsweek, Aug 20, 2009

11   *studies show that, while social media:* http://www.mikekarnj.com/blog/2008/08/05/social-isolation/

11   *40 percent less often compared with 1965:* "Social Isolation Growing in U.S., Study Says," *Washington Post,* June 23, 2006

11   *recent survey found that more than two-thirds:* "Listen to Your Mother; Put That Cell Phone Away and Eat Your Dinner!" http://www.retrevo.com/

12   *concluding that Americans underestimate the power: Thrive: Finding Happiness The Blue Zones Way By Dan Buettner*

13   *her circle of relationships:* "Perinatal Experiences: The Association of Stress, Childbearing, Breastfeeding, and Early Mothering," PMCID: PMC1595161

15   *expert at London's Imperial College, underlines:* "Stress in the womb can last a lifetime, say researchers behind new exhibit," http://esciencenews.com, June 30, 2009

15   *Her statement is based on a study:* "Antenatal maternal stress and long-term effects on child neurodevelopment: how and why?" PMID: 17355398

15   *when mothers experienced marital discord:* "Follow-up study from birth of the effects of prenatal stresses," PMID: 4129091

15   *if they were cruelly treated:* " Maternal stress during pregnancy predicts cognitive ability and fearfulness in infancy," PMID: 18049295

CHAPTER 2: HOW KIDS PICK UP ON EVERYTHING, PART 1—IN THE WOMB

19   *The Council is quite clear*: paper #3 "Excessive Stress Disrupts Architecture of the Developing Brain," http://developingchild. harvard.edu

21   *Harvard's National Scientific Council explains:* Working Paper #6 "Mental Health Problems in Early Childhood Can Impair Learning and Behavior for Life," http://developingchild.harvard.edu

22   *In her review of the research*: "Antenatal maternal stress and long-term effects on child neurodevelopment: how and why?" PMID: 17355398

23   *the first prenatal clinic*: "Emotional factors in prenatal...," PMID: 5320604

23   *This is likely an evolutionary legacy*: "Annual Research Review: Prenatal stress and the origins of psychopathology...," PMID: 21250994

24   *depression have at least one factor in common*: "Stress: Constant stress puts your health at risk," http://www.mayoclinic.com/health/stress/ SR00001

24   *She then compared them to a group*: "How the First Nine Months Shape the Rest of Your Life," *Time Magazine*, Sept. 22, 2010

25   *A review of the scientific literature*: "Practitioner review: early adversity and developmental disorders," PMID: 15845126

25   *In Belgium, a study of:* "High antenatal maternal anxiety is related to ADHD symptoms, externalizing problems, and anxiety in 8- and 9-year-olds," PMID: 15260866

25   *In Canada, a study of 203:* "Relation of maternal stress during pregnancy to symptom severity and response to treatment in children with ADHD," PMCID: PMC2186370

25   *review of the research supporting a non-genetic basis*: "Review: Gestational stress influences...," *Future Neurology* September 2010, Vol. 5, No. 5

26   *we inherit a gene for our eye color*: "Risk factors for autism: perinatal factors, parental psychiatric history, and socioeconomic status," PMID: 15870155

27   *A review of ASD literature*: "Autism spectrum disorders and epigenetics," PMID: 20643313

27   *others give the odds at 70 percent*: "Combined effect of maternal serotonin transporter genotype and prenatal stress in modulating offspring social interaction in mice," PMID: 20470877

27   *or even 30 percent*: "Prenatal stress and risk...," PMCID: PMC2632594

29   *he and his team compared fifteen years*: "Autism prevalence following prenatal exposure to hurricanes and tropical storms in Louisiana," PMID: 17619130

31   *other studies suggest that a baby*: Prenatal stress and risk for autism," PMCID: PMC2632594

31   *his colleagues studied 188 families*: "Timing of prenatal stressors and autism," PMID: 16134032

31   *As he wrote in a 2008 review article*: "Prenatal stress and risk for autism," PMCID: PMC2632594

CHAPTER 3: HOW KIDS PICK UP ON EVERYTHING, PART 2—AFTER A CHILD IS BORN

34   *In experiments when scientists have blocked*: Sarah Hrdy, *Mother Nature: A History of Mothers, Infants, and Natural Selection* (New York: Pantheon, 1999), p. 153-154

35   *Studies have shown the power of a mother's*: Jack Nitschke et al., "*Orbitofrontal Cortex Tracks Positive Mood in Mothers Viewing Pictures of Their Newborn Infants*," NeuroImage 21 (2004), pp. 583-92

35   *that this empathy is mutual*: "Intentional attunement: mirror neurons and the neural underpinnings of interpersonal relations," PMID: 17432495

35   *Nature has equipped him with the ability*: "The neuroscience of human relationships: Attachment and the developing social brain," Cozolino, Louis, New York, NY, US: W W Norton & Co. (2006)

35   *from birds to monkeys*: Daniel Goleman, *Social Intelligence*, p. 215

36   *care will continue as long as possible*: Sarah Hrdy, *Mother Nature*, p. 536

36   *study and analyze this subconscious*: Daniel Stern, *The Interpersonal World of the Infant* (New York: Basic Books, 1987), p. 30

36   *That's why, even in the womb*: Sarah Hrdy, *Mother Nature* p. 379

37   *so as to strengthen that connection*: Sarah Hrdy, *Mother Nature* p. 388

37   *John Cacioppo conducted a large study*: *Social Intelligence: The New Science of Human Relationships* by Daniel Goleman

38   *a study led by Dr. A. Clavarino*: "Maternal anxiety and attention problems in children at 5 and 14 years," PMID: 19805622

38   *A 2002 review by Dr. Rena Repetti*: "Risky Families: Family Social Environments and the Mental and Physical Health...,"PMID:11931522

42   *Harvard and Duke geneticists reported*: "Genes Show Limited Value in Predicting Diseases," *New York Times*, April 15, 2009

42   *Council on the Developing Child states*: "paper #6 Early Experiences can Alter Gene Expression and Affect Long-Term Development," http://developingchild.harvard.edu

43   *In a recent review of the research*: "Epigenetic approaches to psychiatric disorders," PMID: 20373664

43   *Council on the Developing Child states:* "Paper #10, Early Experiences Can Alter Gene Expression and Affect Long-Term Development," developingchild.harvard.edu

44   *Duke geneticist David Goldstein*: "Genes Show Limited Value in Predicting Diseases," *New York Times*, April 15, 2009

45   *National Institutes of Health pledged*: "Epigenetics research takes aim at cancer, Alzheimer's, autism, other illnesses," December 15, 2009

46   *Most Highly Cited Scientist*: http://en.wikipedia.org/wiki/Institute_for_Scientific_Information

46   *Dr. Meaney's pioneering research*: "Epigenetics and the environmental regulation of the genome and its function," PMID: 19958180

46   *But in his research with rats*: "Maternal care and DNA methylation of a glutamic acid decarboxylase 1 promoter in rat...," PMID: 20881131

46   *Harvard's National Scientific Council wrote:* paper #3 "Excessive Stress Disrupts the Architecture of the Developing Brain," http://developingchild.harvard.edu

46   *as first reported by scientists at Berkeley*: "Stressed-out moms, Stressed-out kids," http://sph.berkeley.edu

47   *Berkeley School of Public Health writes: ibid.*

48   *He describes licking only as an "environmental signal"*: "Epigenetics and the environmental regulation of the genome...," PMID: 19958180

49   *Ellen Galinsky discovered:* "Till Children Do Us Part," *New York Times*, February 4, 2009

50   *reported in a pioneering 2004 study*: "Epigenetic programming by maternal behavior," PMID: 15220929

50   *In another article, Dr. Meaney describes*: "Epigenetics and parental effects," PMID: 20652892

51   *Dr. Grafodatskaya concludes:* "Autism spectrum disorders and epigenetics,"

PMID: 20643313

51   *Simon Gregory has found:* "Genomic and epigenetic evidence for oxytocin receptor deficiency in autism," PMCID: PMC2774338

52   *One study in particular offers parents:* "Combined effect of maternal serotonin transporter genotype and prenatal stress in modulating offspring social interaction in mice," PMID: 20470877

53   *From his research on mice, Dr. Potash:* "Chronic Stress May Cause Long-Lasting Epigenetic Changes," http://www.hopkinsmedicine.org

54   *As Dr. Curt Sandman argues:* "Review: Gestational stress influences cognition and behavior," *Future Neurology* September 2010, Vol. 5, No. 5

55   *'goose bumps right now talking about it,':* "DNA referees," *Los Angeles Times,* May 03, 2010

55   *launched the National Children's Study:* http://www.nationalchildrensstudy. gov

56   *Experts estimate that:* "Prenatal stress and risk for autism," PMCID: PMC2632594

56   *Harvard research also points out:* "Economic, neurobiological, and behavioral perspectives on building America's future workforce," and "Roots of Adult Disease Traced to Early Childhood...," developingchild.harvard.edu

CHAPTER 5: PARENTAL STRESS AFFECTS ALMOST EVERY CHILD— IT'S JUST A MATTER OF DEGREE

58   *last 15 years to become an epidemic:* "Is later obesity programmed in utero?: PMID: 17691929

58   *a child's genes that influence obesity:* "Developmental and epigenetic pathways to obesity: an evolutionary-developmental perspective," PMID: 19136993

58   *programming its metabolism to absorb:* "Developmental programming of obesity in mammals," PMID: 17170060

59   *one study of more than 65,000:* "Prenatal Stress Exposure Related to Maternal Bereavement and Risk of Childhood Overweight," PMCID: PMC2912844

59   *result is that obesity-prone babies:* "Is later obesity programmed in utero?" PMID: 17691929

59   *the fetus can be duped:* "Mechanisms underlying the role of glucocorticoids

in the early life programming of adult disease," PMID: 17663659

59 *called the "predictive adaptive response*: "Predictive adaptive responses and human evolution," PMID: 16701430

60 *so important that it bears repeating*: "Prenatal Stress And Risk For Autism," PMCID: PMC2632594

60 *parental stress has been linked to asthma:* Working Paper #6 "Mental Health Problems in Early Childhood Can Impair Learning and Behavior for Life," and Working Paper #3, "Excessive Stress Disrupts the Architecture of the Developing Brain," developingchild.harvard.edu

61 *such as colic, learning disabilities, and allergies:* "Association between life stress during pregnancy and infant crying in the first six months postpartum," PMID: 16472948, and "Prenatal stress and neurodevelopment of the child: focus on the HPA axis and role of the placenta," PMID: 19546565, and "Mother's prenatal stress predisposes their babies to asthma and allergy," e! Science News, May 18, 2008

61 *The experiment found:* "Review: Gestational stress influences cognition and behavior," *Future Neurology* September 2010, Vol. 5, No. 5

62 *in 2002, a review:* "Risky Families: Family Social Environments and the Mental and Physical Health of Offspring," PMID: 11931522

66 *recently demonstrated how prenatal stress:* "High pregnancy anxiety during mid-gestation is associated with decreased gray matter density in 6-9 year-old children," PMCID: PMC2795128

67 *Dr. Sandman concludes:* "Review: Gestational stress influences cognition and behavior," Future Neurology September 2010, Vol. 5, No. 5

68 *They found "strong and significant links":* "Maternal antenatal anxiety and children's behavioural/emotional problems at 4 years," PMID: 12042228

68 *Kennedy Krieger's database showed:* "Cyber Scout Puts Autism Studies On Faster Track," NPR.org

68 *Julie Daniels of UNC Chapel Hill published:* "Parental psychiatric disorders associated with autism spectrum disorders in...," PMID: 18450879

68 *clear that depressed mothers:* #8: "Maternal Depression Can Undermine the Development of Young Children," http://developingchild.harvard.edu

69 *And more than one study has confirmed:* "Prenatal and perinatal risk factors for autism in China," PMID: 20358271 and "Obstetric and parental psychiatric variables as potential predictors of autism severity," PMID: 18324467 and "Prenatal exposure to maternal depression and cortisol

influences infant temperament," PMID: 17513986

70　*one by scientists at the University of Queensland*: "Depression following marital problems: different impacts on mothers and their children? A 21-year prospective study," PMID: 20574844

71　*Council uses the stress of maternal depression*: "Prenatal exposure to maternal depression and cortisol influences infant temperament," PMID: 17513986 and "Working Paper #6 "Mental Health Problems in Early Childhood Can Impair Learning and Behavior...," http://developingchild.harvard.edu

71　*Moshe Szyf wrote that the increase of asthma*: "Epigenetics, Behaviour, and Health," PMCID: PMC2869339

72　*their team set out to analyze the cases*: "Mothers' anxiety during pregnancy is associated with asthma in their children," PMCID: PMC2726292

73　*a 2007 study and 2008 review*: "Prenatal maternal stress and early caregiving experiences: implications for childhood asthma risk," PMID: 17935570 and "Stress and childhood asthma risk: overlapping evidence from animal studies and epidemiologic research," PMID: 20525123

73　*They found that, for mothers who tested*: "Early parental and child predictors of recurrent abdominal pain at school age: results of a large population-based study," PMID: 16721323

CHAPTER 6: STRESS OUTSIDE THE WOMB

75　*his team monitored the stress*: "Association of family stress with natural killer cell activity and the frequency of illnesses in children," PMID: 17339503

75　*Rosalind Wright of Harvard studied 114 families*: "Chronic caregiver stress and IgE expression, allergen-induced proliferation, and cytokine profiles in a birth cohort predisposed to atopy," PMID: 15208584

76　*Dr. Von Korff went on to publish the results*: "Childhood psychosocial stressors and adult onset arthritis," PMID: 19464800

76　*a study of 4,400 families*: "Psychological stress may induce diabetes-related autoimmunity in infancy," PMID: 15677781

76　*The experts found that high stress:* "Psychological stress may induce diabetes-related autoimmunity in infancy," PMID: 15677781

77　*Vulnerable Child Syndrome*: There are over 300 articles on VCS at: http://www.ncbi.nlm.nih.gov/pubmed?term=Vulnerable%20Child%20

Syndrome

80 *In 2001, Susan Dominus reported*: "The Allergy Prison," *New York Times*, June 10, 2001

81 *A recent massive study*: "Food Allergies Common among Children and Linked to Environmental Allergies and Asthma Later in Life, Suggests Largest-Ever National Allergy Study" http://ir.questdiagnostics.com

81 *up to 50 million Americans*: "Airborne Allergens: Something in the Air," http://www.niaid.nih.gov

81 *now affects one in ten children*: http://www.cdc.gov/ncbddd/features/counting-autism.html

81 *She found that children of these anxious mothers*: "Continued exposure to maternal distress in early life is associated with an increased risk of childhood asthma," PMID: 17932381

83 *an infant will be more vulnerable*: #8: "Maternal Depression Can Undermine the Development of Young Children," http://developingchild.harvard.edu

83 *studies suggest that this hypersensitivity*: *The Development Of Autism: Perspectives From Theory And Research* By Jacob A. Burack

83 *page 3:* Working Paper #6 "Mental Health Problems in Early Childhood Can Impair Learning and Behavior...," http://developingchild.harvard.edu

84 *Dr. Panksepp expresses concern*: Jaak Panksepp, *Affective Neuroscience: The Foundations of Human and Animal Emotions*, (New York: Oxford University Press, 1998), p. 320

85 *releases all kinds of bonding hormones*: "Oxytocin, a neuropeptide regulating affection and social behavior," PMID: 21648164 and "First-borns carry a higher metabolic risk in early adulthood: evidence from a prospective cohort study," PMID: 21085691

85 *she throws herself into her new relationship*: "Neuroendocrine perspectives on social attachment and love," PMID: 9924738 and http://en.wikipedia.org/wiki/Human_bonding

86 *Dr. T. Berry Brazelton, writes*: "Family pattern stirs concern about over-mothered child," Albany Times Union, August 29, 2007

86 *author Judith Warner writes*: Judith Warner, *Perfect Madness: Motherhood in the Age of Anxiety* (New York: Riverhead Books, 2005), p. 133

87 *Council for the Developing Child states*: Working Paper #9 "Persistent Fear and Anxiety Can Affect Young Children's Learning and Development,"

http://developingchild.harvard.edu

89   *Researchers in Italy and England*: "First-borns carry a higher metabolic risk in early adulthood: evidence from a prospective...," PMID: 21085691

89   *more first-borns have problems*: "Firstborn Kids Seem to Have More Food Allergies, Hay Fever," http://www.medicinenet.com

89   *Regarding enmeshment, research suggests*: "Neuroendocrine and emotional changes in the post-partum period," PMID: 11589134

89   *Although research on this area*: "Primigravid and Multigravid Women: Prenatal Perspectives," PMCID: PMC1893079

90   *"Why Do Siblings Turn Out Differently?"*: Available at the Bowen Center for the Study of the Family

CHAPTER 7: OUR DWINDLING SOCIAL NETWORKS LEAVE PARENTS MORE STRESSED THAN EVER

95   *at the core of our being, as research confirms*: "Stress, social support, and the buffering hypothesis," Cohen, Sheldon; Wills, Thomas A. *Psychological Bulletin*, Vol 98(2), Sep 1985, 310-357

96   *He writes that there is an epidemic*: "Why is there so much depression today? The waxing of the individual and the waning of the commons," by Martin Seligman, from *Contemporary Psychological Approaches To Depression*, Ingram, Rick E. (Ed), (1990).

96   *we have become, and researchers in various other institutes have come to the same conclusion*:
      "Adapting to College Life In an Era of Heightened Stress," *New York Times*, August 06, 2000, "Age-cohort changes in the lifetime occurrence of depression and other mental disorders," PMID: 8436687,
      "Increasing rates of depression," PMID: 2648043,
      "National patterns in antidepressant medication...," PMID: 19652124
      "Further Examining the American Dream: Differential Correlates of Intrinsic and Extrinsic Goals," Record- EJ525659 at ERIC.ed.gov

96   *Dr. Twenge notes*: "The age of anxiety? Birth cohort change in anxiety and neuroticism, 1952-1993," PMID: 11138751

96   *psychiatric patients in the 1950s*: "A comparison of parental and self-evaluations of psychopathology in children," PMID: 14416337

97   *What the USC team found*: "Parental stress and childhood wheeze in a prospective cohort study" PMID: 18446597

98   *a large body of medical literature*: "Social relationships and health," PMID: 15554821 and "Assessing The Physical Health Aspects Of Social Networks And Social Support," Ann. Rev. Public Health, 1984 5:413-32

98   *Again, Dr. Twenge*: "The age of anxiety? Birth cohort change in anxiety and neuroticism, 1952-1993," PMID: 11138751

98   *social grooming has increased*: "The need to belong: Desire for interpersonal attachments as a fundamental human motivation," Baumeister, Roy F.; Leary, Mark R. *Psychological Bulletin*, Vol 117(3), May 1995, 497-529

99   *A review by scientists at Cornell*: "Increasing rates of depression," PMID: 2648043

99   *Authors of the study*: "Social Isolation in America: Changes in Core Discussion Networks over Two Decades," by Miller McPherson, Lynn Smith-Lovin, Matthew E. Brashears

99   *Dr. Twenge also describes*: "It's beyond my control: a cross-temporal meta-analysis of increasing externality in locus of control...," PMID: 15454351

99   *alienation among Americans, asserting*: "Birth cohort increases in psychopathology among young Americans, 1938-2007: A cross-temporal meta-analysis of the MMPI," PMID: 19945203

102   *she began seeing a physician*: John Sarno, MD: Healing Back Pain: The Mind-Body Connection

CHAPTER 8: TODAY'S PARENTS HAVE GONE PRIMAL

105   *Associated Press-Ipsos poll*: "Associated Press: Rudeness Study," conducted by Ipsos Public Affairs, August 25, 2005

105   *In a 2002 survey*: http://www.publicagenda.org/files/pdf/aggravating_circumstances.pdf

105   *told Public Agenda pollsters*: www.publicagenda.org/files/pdf/teaching_interrupted.pdf

105   *New York Times column*: "THE NATION; Kids Gone Wild," November 27, 2005

107   *Alvin Rosenfeld explains*: *Ibid.*

107   *Harvard University child psychologist, says*: *Ibid.*

109   *writes in the Washington Post*: "The Irony of Fear," *The Washington Post*, August 30, 2005

unavailability and children's adjustment difficulties," PMID: 17107450

126 *2009 New York Times article*: "Fathers Gain Respect From Experts (and Mothers)," *The New York Times*, November 2, 2009

126 *Fragile Families and Child Wellbeing Study*: fragilefamilies.princeton.edu

128 *The results of this study*: "Fathers' and mothers' marital relationship predicts daughters' pubertal development two years later," PMID: 18706686

CHAPTER 11: MYTH: THE MORE ATTENTION WE GIVE OUR KIDS, THE BETTER THEY TURN OUT

130 *Page 6: Perfect Madness: Motherhood In The Age Of Anxiety* by Judith Warner

131 *studies show that today's parents*: "Surprisingly, Family Time Has Grown, *New York Times*, April 5, 2010

131 *Page 38: Perfect Madness: Motherhood In The Age Of Anxiety* by Judith Warner

133 *"We use kids like Prozac," says*: "THE NATION; Kids Gone Wild," *New York Times*, November 27, 2005

CHAPTER 12: HOW TO REDUCE STRESS BY SOCIALIZING MORE

141 *conducted studies showing that even a brief relationship*: "Effects of family foundations on parents and children: 3.5 years after baseline," PMID: 20954763

141 *can improve the well-being of both parents*: "Effects of family foundations on parents and children: 3.5 years after baseline," PMID: 20954763

146 *We instinctively search for a mate with the same level of anxiety*: "Mating-related interactions share common features with anxiety...," PMID: 17854918

APPENDIX 1: FURTHER EVIDENCE OF THE MIND-BODY CONNECTION BETWEEN PARENT AND CHILD

156 *There are also many studies*: "Maternal antenatal anxiety and behavioural/ emotional problems in children: a test of a programming hypothesis," PMID: 14531585

156 *one study in Belgium*: "High antenatal maternal anxiety is related to

ADHD symptoms, externalizing problems, and anxiety in 8- and 9-year-olds," PMID: 15260866

157 *Dr. Ward found previous studies:* "Psychosocial assets, life crisis and the prognosis of pregnancy," PMID: 5021933, and "Prenatal antecedents of child health, development, and behavior. An epidemiological report of incidence and association," PMID: 56345

157 *this study from Yale:* "Psychosocial assets, life crisis and the prognosis of pregnancy," PMID: 5021933

157 *In the journal Medical Hypotheses he notes:* "Prenatal influences on brain dopamine and their relevance to the rising incidence...," PMID: 16959433

157 *ten-fold in the past three decades:* "A comparison and analysis of the presence of family problems during pregnancy of mothers of "autistic" children and mothers of normal children," PMID: 2376213

158 *Dr. Weinstock's review:* "The long-term behavioural consequences of prenatal stress," PMID: 18423592

158 *In a recent review of the medical research:* "Fetal programming: Early-life modulations that affect adult outcomes," PMID: 20617403

159 *a study of 219 babies:* "Neurodevelopmental disability through 11 years of age in children born before 26 weeks of gestation," PMID: 19651566

159 *She also found that childhood anxiety:* "Childhood adversity, early-onset depressive/anxiety disorders, and adult-onset asthma," PMID: 18941133

APPENDIX 2: DR JIONG LI: PRENATAL STRESS INCREASES THE ODDS OF ADHD, BUT NOT AUTISM?

160 *Dr. Li's conclusions differed:* "A nationwide study on the risk of autism after prenatal stress exposure to maternal bereavement," PMID: 19336368

163 *She estimates in her review:* "Antenatal maternal stress and long-term effects on child neurodevelopment: how and why?" PMID: 17355398

163 *based on several different studies:* "Maternal antenatal anxiety and children's behavioural/emotional problems at 4 years," PMID: 12042228, and "Antenatal anxiety predicts child behavioral/emotional problems independently of postnatal depression," PMID: 12447034, and "Maternal antenatal anxiety and behavioural/emotional problems in

children: a test of a programming hypothesis," PMID: 14531585

163 *refuting Dr. Li's interpretation is another study:* "Risk factors for autism: perinatal factors, parental psychiatric history, and...," PMID: 15870155

163 *publish an article:* "Risk factors for autism: perinatal factors, parental psychiatric history, and socioeconomic status," PMID: 15870155

164 *and found that expectant mothers:* "Maternal antenatal anxiety and children's behavioural/emotional problems at 4 years," PMID: 12042228

KIDS PICK UP ON EVERYTHING